Praise for *I've Been Called the B* Word...*
Now What Do I Do?

"Dr. Green has created *the* roadmap to success for women entrepreneurs. Simply amazing."
— Savannah Britt, owner of Girlpez.com

"The *B* Word* tackles the hurdles of being a woman in today's world and offers bold solutions and techniques for getting ahead. Part manual, part inspiration, this book is sure to be a hit."
— Juliette Brindak, cocreator and founder of Miss O
    and Friends

"Dr. Green is a role model for all women in business, from CEOs to new entrepreneurs. We all owe her a debt of gratitude for lighting the way."
— Kanini Mutooni, founder of myAzimia.org
    and inuka.org

"This book is so good, you won't be able to put it down. Packed with practical business advice and sage personal wisdom, it's got something for every woman who wants to redefine herself."
— Rachel Hollis, founder and proprietor of Chic Events

I've Been Called the B* Word...

Now What Do I Do?

I've Been Called the B* Word...
Now What Do I Do?

13 Rules
for the "New-Age" Professional Woman

Dr. R. Kay Green

RKG Marketing Solutions, Inc.

*I've Been Called the B*Word...Now What Do I Do?:*
13 Rules for the "New-Age" Professional Woman
Copyright © 2013 Dr. R. Kay Green
Published by RKG Marketing Solutions, Inc.

For more information contact:
info@rkgmarketingsolutions.com

Please visit www.ivebeencalledthebword.com

Book design by:
www.arborbooks.com

Printed in the United States of America

*I've Been Called the B*Word...Now What Do I Do?:*
13 Rules for the "New-Age" Professional Woman
Dr. R. Kay Green

1. Title   2. Author   3. Business/Marketing

Library of Congress Control Number: 2012912408

ISBN 13: 978-0-9858901-0-0

Dedication

This book is dedicated to the many individuals I have encountered on my life's journey. I am a firm believer that is it no coincidence who we encounter and at what point in our lives we encounter them.

To Greg Hagin, CPA, who one day, on a routine appointment, helped brainstorm the title of a speaking engagement that has coincidently become the title of this book.

To Dr. Barbara Bart and Dr. Emily Crawford, who provided a solid undergraduate foundation and an understanding of marketing as a base to begin my career.

To Sam Crossley, my first mentor, who taught me the value of understanding customer relationships.

To Dr. Victor Williams, my doctoral mentor, who raised the question, "How will you contribute the field of marketing?"

To my dad, Roger Green, who has always been my greatest source of support, and who never limited what I could accomplish and the possibilities that would evolve.

Finally to Kennedy Channing, my greatest source of inspiration, who informs me every day that I have inspired someone.

The primary goal I want to accomplish in life is to inspire someone…to challenge what is and consider what can be.

—Dr. R. Kay Green

Table of Contents

The B Word

We've all heard it. Whether it was spoken about us or about someone we knew, we've been there. A few times (okay, maybe even more than a few times) we've said it about someone else. We've seen the effect the word can have. That demeaning, debasing, and sometimes crippling word—the all-powerful B word. A quick check of the dictionary entry for this word shows a colorful array of definitions befitting a term with an extraordinarily colorful history. For more than 600 years, the traditional B word has evolved from a simple descriptor into the wide range of derogatory uses it occupies today.

But why does it have so much power over women in particular? Certainly it has a great deal to do with the disparaging original meaning. It was (and is) suggestive of lewdness, crudeness, and even looseness. At its height it was considered the most offensive thing a person could call a woman. These are all truths, but they don't even scratch the surface of why I believe the B word is such a damaging thing for a woman—particularly for a woman in business.

I've been called many things in my life, but the B word holds more sway than any of them. Why? Not because it is profane and insulting but because, for a woman in business, it is often applied as a label simply because of your status or position. No matter what you do—no matter how effective or how kind or how selfless you are—in business and in life you may be called the B word at some point. Interestingly, a woman's propensity to be branded with the word seems to be commensurate with her level of success.

As I reflected on my personal experiences in business, I found I had been called many B words throughout my career. In fact, as I thought about the B word concept, it occurred to me that one B word could hardly describe any one woman in business. I thought of the many other B words I had been called: believer, bold, brilliant, businesslike, brainy, brave, blessed, beautiful, and busy. It seemed to me that, considering the sheer number of positive B words out there, with the right frame of mind a professional woman could always find better perspectives on what the traditional B word means.

Right around the time that I first began to develop the concept for this book, it occurred to me that someone should write a manual about how to find success in business despite the nearly inevitable B word label. I thought for a moment that maybe I was alone. Maybe there are thousands of women who find surpassing success—whether at their nine-to-five jobs or in their entrepreneurial ventures—without ever being branded a B word. Being the researcher I am, I figured if I planned to spin my hypothesis around the inescapability of the B word, I should probably test its feasibility.

So I scoured the web and as many publications as I could locate in search of twelve women entrepreneurs who might be able to share their thoughts on my theory. I knew that no matter what the outcome of the interview series I planned with these women, I would need to draw from as diverse a set of experiences as possible. I couldn't interview twelve women just like me—otherwise my hypothesis might seem biased. No, I needed women from greatly different backgrounds, of a wide range of ages, and blessed with differing paths to the tops of their respective fields. And that is exactly what I found.

In my interviews with these twelve incredibly skilled and wonderfully successful women, I discovered that my hypothesis was certainly correct. Though these women demonstrated great diversity in personality and life experience, all of them had been called quite a few different B words. No, I was certainly not alone. It appeared that most successful women hear many different B words over the courses of their careers—and yes, sometimes the B word in question is the traditional derogatory B word. You might not hear that dreaded word often; you might not even hear it directly; but if you ever climb the corporate ladder or come to dominate the market with your business, you will eventually hear it in some form or another. In many ways, if you are a woman who aspires to success, the B word is the unjust and sometimes humiliating culmination of all things.

When I realized that my hypothesis had value, I decided it was indeed time to write my manual for women in business. I knew I wanted to empower my readers. I wanted to give them something to stand up and get excited about. I wanted to take the traditional concept of the B word and put a new-age spin on it—empowering women to embrace all the B words they have ever been called, and demonstrating ways to make the B word work *for them* instead of against them.

I don't have to tell you the world is changing. Every day, new developments in technology and society rewrite the rulebooks for how we interact with our families, our colleagues, and our customers. The world gets smaller with each new development. And with that shrinking of the planet comes a new sense and celebration of diversity and individuality. More than ever before, women are climbing the corporate ladder. More than ever before, women are achieving greatness by way of their startup companies. More than ever before, a male professional can look a female professional in the eye and see at least something akin to an equal. But, despite all this change, the traditional B word remains.

It's time to reclaim the word. Time to shred it of its meaning. Time to replace it with a new series of empowering, positive, and infinitely more descriptive B words. This book attempts to do just that, in addition to providing modern solutions to modern business problems. In my interviews with the twelve women who contributed to this book, I first asked them to provide ten B words that described them. The responses I received were informative, insightful, and always very authentic. The experience of replacing that all too common B word with a range of positive B words proved remarkably cathartic for all of us. And it proved to me once and for all that professional women are so much more than the labels they may have picked up along the way.

Before I offer up my summary of the real-life solutions this book provides, let's meet the women, shall we? As I mentioned, each of these women comes from a very different background, but they all share one important thing: they were daring enough to achieve tremendous success in their fields. Some started companies. Some developed concepts that became cultural phenomena. Some contribute to the arts. They have excelled in fashion and finance and sport. They have found great success in their careers, and though they all followed different paths to that success, they share a number of traits, insights, and strategies common to dynamic entrepreneurs.

When asked about the ten positive B words that best described her, award-winning entrepreneur and women's success coach Erica Diamond suggested she is bold, bright, blessed, brave, bubbly, bullish, buoyant, businesslike, a believer, and brunette. And, as I would find during our interview, the words could not have been more apt. As a forward thinker who always puts her family first, Erica has found great success in part because she has never doubted herself.

"I grew up as an only child doing another play of entrepreneurship every day," she told me. "I was always pretending to own something. A store. A restaurant. Anything that had me working for myself and calling the shots."

That spirit has carried her well throughout her life, and has led to her award-winning career in a variety of entrepreneurial ventures from a promotional-products company to her incredibly inspiring blog, WomenOnTheFence.com.

Celebrity photographer Drexina Nelson described herself as business-oriented, blessed, bright, bold, blissful, bull-headed, bureaucratic, balanced, brave, and buoyant. I found that last word struck a particular chord for us both, given that she and I have endured paths that have caused us to change direction a number of times. A belief in dreams is always the top motivator for a successful woman in business, but during those times when the tide gets high, it helps to be able to keep your head above water. Drexina's path took her from earning an undergraduate degree in art to living as an aspiring artist and then going back to college for her MBA, but even when she landed a corporate job in a leadership development program for the Ford Motor Company, she never gave up the dream to contribute to the arts. "I grew up reading *Vogue*," she told me. "Everything I've done has led me to where I am today." Drexina is one of the most celebrated and skilled photographers in Atlanta (www.drexina. com), and there seems no limit to where her art can take her.

Born in Kenya, Kanini Mutooni, founder of microfinance companies myAzimia.org and inuka.org, described herself as a believer, brilliant, businesslike, better, black, bullish, burgeoning, brave, bouncy, and blessed. Though her path has taken her away from her native Africa, she has long been driven by a desire to open up avenues for business on the continent (which represents the remarkable power behind myAzimia.org) and give back to women in business (the primary goal of inuka.org). Her ventures have taken her from Kenya to London to Jersey and now to Germany, but no matter where she has landed she has managed to exact great change for her employers, herself, and her own companies.

"I pride myself on being able to be successful in whichever environment I am in," she told me. That adaptability and uncommon drive makes her a shining example of how giving back can sometimes be the truest path to achievement.

Trainer and business consultant Ana Cortés described herself as brilliant, beautiful, buxom, best, brave, and balanced. I can certainly attest to her bravery and balance. After paying her way through university in Mexico, marrying at a young age, and then finding herself living as a single mother of two, Ana began her life as an entrepreneur out of a sheer need to provide for her children.

"I had to try to do things I didn't know I was able to do," she shared. At the age of twenty-seven, she started her first business, and the venture sparked in her a passion for entrepreneurship that led to a series of additional businesses in Mexico and eventually the United States. The way Ana managed to balance such a workload with motherhood is a truly remarkable story, but even as she juggled the many responsibilities such a thing requires, she was winning awards, launching successful startups, and changing lives for the better.

Rachel Hollis, founder and proprietor of Chic Events, a high-level event planning company, owns such B words as blessed, bright, believer, burgeoning, buoyant, bubbly, bold, busy, brave, and brazen. Having grown up in a small town in California, her venture into elite party planning has turned into a career that seems worlds apart from her upbringing. But that brazen spirit is exactly what has led Chic Events to reach such great heights.

"There's an aspect of event planning that is the same as a stage play," she explained. "You're doing all this buildup and practice for something that only lasts one night." You have to be confident, bold, in order to pull off such a tenuous thing. But it is perhaps Rachel's infectious confidence that has propelled the success of her business. "Starting my own company came from a place of not wanting to work for jerks or kill myself to promote somebody else's career. I decided on the spur of the moment to quit my job on a Friday. I started Chic Events on a Monday." And the rest is history.

Bold, beautiful, brilliant, and brave Savannah Britt, a remarkable young woman who was at one time the youngest magazine publisher in the world, has been working in the writing and publishing industry since the tender age of nine. That GirlPez. com has evolved into one of the most popular and successful fashion magazines/blogs in the country is a testament to her willingness to accept any challenge. In many ways her greatest challenge over the years has been overcoming the prejudice often associated with her youth.

"No matter how old you are, you have to be brave when you dive into a business venture," she revealed. "Many potential entrepreneurs tend to hold back. But if you're going to go all in, you have to be willing to take that risk. You have to take that B word 'brave' and run with it."

Juliette Brindak, cocreator and founder of Miss O and Friends, a charming website designed to offer preteen and teen girls a safe and comfortable environment in which to network and socialize, describes herself as blessed, bashful, blonde, believable, blissful, brave, bubbly, and businesslike. Those final two points are what make Juliette such a compelling business-woman. In conversation one can hear the girlish bubbliness that led to the essential authenticity of Miss O and Friends, but it is also quite clear that her natural business acumen is what generated the company's incredible success.

She explained that these two qualities are the direct result of a pair of parents who believed in her idea and her abilities enough to put her in front of venture capitalists to pitch the idea on her own. Keep in mind that Juliette was barely out of middle school at the time the company was launched.

"I've been blessed with a great family dynamic," she explained. "I owe so much to the belief my parents placed in me." The result of that belief—one of the most empowering B words in the bunch—is a successful social networking company led by one of the most capable young women I have ever had the pleasure to meet.

Beauty journalist and editor Tai Beauchamp described herself as bold, brilliant, busy, brave, blessed, business-minded, benevolent, and (my favorite) beauty-full. The latter is a word Tai coined in her writings, a term meant to describe the holistic beauty—not simply the surface beauty—of a woman.

Tai is certainly a beauty-full woman. Her remarkable background began humbly, but thanks to the foresight and determination of her mother and grandmother, she would go on to college and achieve the tremendous success that followed. The all-women environments she experienced over the ensuing years instilled in her a sense of pride in the power of women that led directly to her success as an entrepreneur.

"When women are given the opportunity and placed in environments where they're really taught leadership and service," she pointed out, "they tend to thrive and grow."

Kyle Smitley, founder of Barley & Birch, an organic clothing company geared toward providing children with the safest and most environmentally friendly clothing possible, cited the B words benevolent, bouncy, blunt, bullheaded, bright, ballsy, bossy, bold, beast, and believer. You can see Kyle's occasionally aggressive nature shining through in her B words, and you can hear it in her voice when she discusses the state of the modern children's clothing industry. She is truly passionate about her product, and that passion has vaulted Barley & Birch to the heights it currently enjoys.

But of all the impressions I received from Kyle, it was her benevolence that most impressed me. Having spent time in Haiti as a child and South America as a college student, she knew if she ever managed to launch a successful company, she would want to use the profits to foster good in this world.

"I knew if I would ever be rich, I would want to give back," she said. "I want to make a lot of money for the sole purpose of being able to donate a lot of money." That spirit holds true in her personal actions but also underlies everything her company does.

Prerna Gupta, founder and CEO of Khush, a company that develops intelligent music apps for iPhone and Android, described herself as beautiful, benevolent, blessed, blissful, brainy, brave, businesslike, burgeoning, and bullish. That attitude of always growing and always burgeoning as a person led Prerna from her youth in small-town Oklahoma to her current position as head of one of the most innovative app makers around.

"I had an interesting first two decades of my life because I was of a different religion and race than most other people in Oklahoma," she explained. "But the challenges I faced as a child really helped shape my character, helped to teach me to be strong in my beliefs, understand who I am, and be confident in myself."

Prerna clearly lives this wisdom. Part of why she is so empowered as a businesswoman is that she knows exactly who she is, what she wants, and, most importantly, where she intends to go.

Bobbie Kelsey-Grayson, head women's basketball coach at the University of Wisconsin, describes herself as blessed, bold, bright, blunt, black, brave, bubbly, businesslike, brutal, and bossy. Those final two points are owed to a life of playing and then coaching basketball, a sport that has bred in her an unflinching desire to win. But, according to Bobbie, that competitive fire has always been a part of her nature.

"Basketball just fit my personality," she said. "I've always been drawn to competition, and there's something about the game that calls to me." Her brutal and bossy attitude on the court led to a winning—though injury-shortened—career as a player for Stanford, and has guided her along her path to a job to which she long aspired.

Believer, blessed, brave, benevolent, bright, blunt, business-oriented, boundless, beneficial, and broken-down—these were the words Dina Marto, cofounder of Twelve Music Group, used to describe herself. That final point might come as a shock to some, but as Dina explains, "You have to be broken down to be built back up."

Of Dina's ten words, it came to me as no shock that *believer* was listed first. Dina, after all, has made a name for herself and started a business in an industry that is tough enough for *anyone* to crack, let alone a young woman. Music production is a bit of a boys' club, but no matter where she has gone or who she has worked for, Dina has established herself as a force in the industry. And she owes it all to that intense belief that music is exactly what she was destined to do.

"I knew growing up that I would be in the music business," she revealed. "I didn't know how or where or when, but I knew I would be in music."

What I learned from these amazing businesswomen is that women in business are evolving. They're becoming more multi-dimensional than ever before. Where entrepreneurship—or any position of leadership, for that matter—used to be dominated by men, more and more women are learning to wear all the hats it takes to find that success, and, more importantly, are demonstrating capabilities far surpassing the expectations of anyone who would resort to branding them with the traditional B word. These women found success by embracing their own ranges of more positive B words, and you can achieve similar greatness by doing the same.

In the pages to come, I present you with a new host of B

words built around a tested framework for success in business and in life. With the strategies in this book, you will learn how to ignore the traditional B word label and become a strong and empowered woman in business. You will learn how to reinvent yourself, build your brand, create the right network, dress for your dream job, be relentless in your pursuits, inspire others, self-actualize, and change your perspective on competition. Most importantly you will emerge with the kind of mindset that drove these thirteen women (myself included) to the tops of their industries.

Congratulations on your decision to pursue a higher path in life. Now let us begin the journey.

Embrace the "I'll Show You" Mind Frame

Believer, Belittler, Brash, Bullish, Better

Before we begin our journey together, I would like to ask you to take a quick look inward. One exercise I like to complete each day is a self-assessment of how much effort I have been putting in to all of my daily tasks. Often I will stand in front of the mirror when I complete this exercise. That way I can hold myself accountable for the response. Every day I ask myself this question, and today I invite you to do the same: on a scale from 1 to 100, how much effort are you putting in to achieving your goal?

So where do you reside? Are you a 100? If so you can put this book down. Are you below 50? If so you have some work to do. Are you above 50? That's great; you still have some work to do. Until we find ourselves committing 100 percent to everything we do, we are not committing enough. No matter what your number, and no matter what your goals for the future, I present you with this one simple request: when you read this book, be a 100. Give all of your attention and effort into absorbing the wisdoms contained in this chapter and the chapters to come. I say this not because I feel like you won't be able to succeed without absorbing every word I've written; I say this because one doesn't truly succeed at *anything* without giving 100 percent.

Now, as we move forward, remember your number. Our goal here will be to figure out the best ways to bring that number up. By the end of the book, if you haven't yet reached 100, you will at least have everything you need to continue the journey toward that ultimate goal.

Let's begin…

I was never good at being an employee. I'm just not the kind of person who fits the typical forty-hour week. So to those who knew me, it shouldn't have come as a shock when I first took the leap and quit my standard nine-to-five job. But back then, when I told people I was quitting and had no intention of going back, many seemed to think I'd gone crazy. I had merely explained I was withdrawing from the security of my chosen career in favor of the pursuit of other professional interests, but some of the people in my life reacted as if I were planning on joining the circus or taking up treasure hunting on the beach.

I discovered early on that these few (but outspoken) people were my Belittlers—my doubters, the otherwise well-intentioned friends and coworkers who would seek to undercut my dreams. As a Believer—one who aspired to do great things against all odds—I knew immediately that I had two choices: I could either allow my Belittlers to drag me away from my dream, or I could use their doubt as fuel for my desire to turn them into Believers like me.

The traditional American dream is kind of a double-edged sword. Certainly it inspires many people to achieve great things. At the same time, it has become so uniform and so well-entrenched that most people can't seem to wrap their minds around the thought of diverting even slightly from the prescribed path. We all learn from a very young age the importance of education, a house, and a steady, reasonably well-paying job, and most people aspire to that dream with intense focus. Then there are the rest of us. We grow up with dreams of blazing our own trails to success through entrepreneurship or innovation. Where many would follow a predefined path to happiness, we prefer to go our own way. Still, even a large percentage of we Believers eventually find our hopes cut down by those constant reminders that there's nothing quite like the safety of a nine-to-six.

Imagine you've just graduated from college with a bachelor's degree in marketing. Say you've landed what many might call a great job in the marketing department at Coca-Cola. Like most recent college grads, you find yourself having to start somewhere near the bottom of the pyramid. You're just one step up from the mailroom, you're so new to the job. Subscribers to the traditional American dream would be content to work that job as hard as they could in the hope they would one day be promoted. Then, once promoted, they would do the same in the hope of being promoted again. But not you. You are a Believer. You have decided you see yourself as the ideal candidate to fill the job of brand manager for the entire company, and the only way you're going to be able to do that before you reach the ripe old age of thirty is to broaden your skillset and branch out from your current role.

The Belittlers would tell you that you're aiming too high. They would remind you that, as brand manager for Coca-Cola, you would be serving one of the most important roles for one of the most recognizable brands on the planet. Essentially you would be one of the most powerful and influential people in the global marketing landscape. This is the kind of career reserved for seasoned veterans, not naïve Believers straight out of college.

Where many would tell you the best course of action when encountering this kind of negative energy would be to ignore it, this chapter takes the concept one step further. We should not simply ignore the negative energy of our Belittlers; we should *use* it as leverage for our determination to succeed.

When I first encountered my Belittlers, I decided I was going to embrace a new mindset. I could have folded. I could have caved in. I could have listened to the Belittlers who warned that it would be crazy to go off on my own. But I didn't. Instead I used every negative comment and word of warning as fuel for my passion to achieve my dream. I embraced what I like to call the "I'll Show You" Mind Frame. I decided that every time someone told me I couldn't, it would only reinforce my belief that I could. Every shred of negative energy from that day forward would serve to increase my desire to succeed.

The "I'll Show You" Mind Frame allows you to succeed in spite of the most frequent drags on your dreams. It drives you to work on your skills, think positively, and internalize what it is you want to do. It leads you to develop a blueprint for how to become that brand manager while you're still in your twenties— or whatever other lofty goal you might have in mind. It gets you away from the kind of thinking that generates doubt, and launches you into the mindset of possibility. You go from worrying about your lack of skills to figuring out ways to develop those skills. You go from wondering how you will ever be able to make the connections you need to going out and actually making them. Doubt becomes motivation. Motivation becomes action. Action leads to dreams realized. Every single time.

It's Not About Getting Even

It's easy to mistake the "I'll Show You" Mind Frame for having a chip on your shoulder. It's even easier to fall into that trap of turning negative into negative. Many people, when told by their Belittlers that they aren't going to make it on their chosen paths to success, react with equal negativity. They allow those words of doubt to anger them or fuel a desire to get even. Achieving their dreams becomes more a matter of proving Belittlers wrong than proving themselves right. In a sense they allow the negativity to make Belittlers of themselves.

Why is this an important distinction to point out? Because your dreams aren't about your Belittlers and what they think; your dreams are about *you*. The more time and energy you spend on worrying about proving other people wrong, the less time and energy you have to dedicate to meeting the milestones on your blueprint. If you focus on disproving your Belittlers, you lose focus on what you have to do in the here and now.

The "I'll Show You" Mind Frame isn't about getting mad or even. It's about changing your way of thinking. It's about

increasing your determination to be better,
smarter, and more efficient with literally
everything you do. It's about using that negative energy as motivation not to disprove
others, but rather to improve yourself.

⸺

For me the new mind frame paid off quickly. Once I finally took
the leap, I figured out where my strengths lay. I gained a new
sense of self, born of the freedom that comes with going your
own way. Determining that you can do something—against all
odds and despite all doubters—has a way of teaching you who
you really are because the work you are doing is for you, and not
for a company that demands work from you.

As a result my self-confidence increased dramatically. I
began to trust myself in ways I never could have imagined
before. I became less afraid to fail. I learned to survive with a
little, and then learned to survive with a lot. Truly I had realized
the benefits of jumping off the ledge and then figuring out how
to build the airplane on the way down.

Externally the rewards were substantial as well. When I
began to find some success, I gained the recognition and appre-
ciation of the friends and coworkers who once had doubted me.
And though I wasn't really in it for the money, the money did
come. I tripled my former income within the first year.

With the twelve successful women interviewed for this book,
the "I'll Show You" Mind Frame arose from different circumstances but almost always came as the result of difficult times
in their lives. Many people, when they meet with tough times,
fold and even accept failure. The women I interviewed for this

book are not among them. Their difficult experiences led them to change course, strive harder, and do whatever it took to show their doubters they could do anything they put their minds to.

Take Kanini Mutooni of myAzimia.org for example. Having grown up in Kenya, the prescribed mind frame came with the territory.

"All of the decisions I made from the age of twelve onward were based on my desire to be in business," she told me. "There was never a time in my life when I was confused about what I was going to do." It was exactly this spirit that allowed her to travel from her home country to become an established businesswoman and then establish a company designed to give back to the community from which she'd come. "If you don't visualize yourself achieving your dreams, you actually won't be able to achieve them."

Sometimes the Mind Frame is born of necessity. According to trainer and business consultant Ana Cortés, "Around the age of twenty-five, I found myself with a one-year-old and a one-week-old. Having those kids meant I didn't have an excuse to fail." For her, success was a matter of survival. Visualizing that future became that much more important as a result. "I think to get to where you need to be, you have to visualize yourself there. Maybe I couldn't see the details at the time, but I knew that there was a bigger me."

This is exactly the kind of success to which the Mind Frame leads—a kind of success that is remarkably repeatable if you learn to turn all negative energy into positive energy. It leads to the discovery of more creative ways to meet your challenges. It introduces an ability to overcome the most trying times. It helps you to turn setbacks into giant leaps forward. Most importantly the "I'll Show You" Mind Frame allows you to take what you're good at and maximize it—and when you can maximize those things at which you excel, a whole world of doors begins to open.

So how do we move toward a positive and productive "I'll Show You" Mind Frame? By absorbing and adhering to the following steps:

1. **Don't listen to your negative thinking.**
   Before I landed my first job, I endured a great many unsuccessful interviews. Sometimes I didn't get the position because I was too young. Sometimes it seemed I was overqualified. Still other times I just "wasn't the right fit." Eventually all this rejection began to pile up in my mind. It wasn't long before I began to notice that the way I talked to myself and thought about myself had become painfully negative. I had begun to tell myself I wasn't getting these jobs because I just wasn't good enough or didn't have the right education. The way I interacted within my own mind had become incredibly damaging.

   At the start of this chapter, I provided insight into how our Belittlers can be destructive forces when it comes to the pursuit of our dreams. Well, there is no more destructive Belittler than ourselves. Negative thoughts can take us to levels of doubt that negative words can never hope to reach. This is because negative words are just words. They can be ignored. They can be shaped. They can be used for the greater good. But negative thoughts are far more difficult to escape. If we listen to them—or, worse, allow them to dominate our Mind Frame—then they become the soundtrack to our efforts. When that happens, failure is never far away.

To think negatively is to believe negatively. And if you believe negatively, you have very little hope of achieving your dreams. For this reason, the first and most important step toward building the "I'll Show You" Mind Frame is to work on ways to ignore your negative thoughts. There are many proven methods; it's just a matter of trying them out to see which work for you.

Whenever you notice you are thinking negatively, you might consider doing something to distract your mind, like reading up on a subject or skill you will need in the pursuit of your dream. You might consider bombarding your mind with positive memories. You might try meditation or some other physical or mental trigger that can remove you from the negative train of thought and get you back on a more productive path. Some people prefer to write down all of their negative thoughts and then counteract them by writing down more positive alternatives.

Whatever the case, you need to develop a working method that will help you to eliminate negative thought and/or turn it positive. But you can't do any of this until you identify what your negative thoughts sound like. They can be sneaky. It didn't occur to me that I was thinking negatively during the interview process until the day I showed up for one with slumped shoulders, a conventional suit, and a gloomy demeanor. This wasn't me. I've always been a positive, can-do kind of person. But there I was, walking into an interview like it was my own funeral.

I realized at that point I had allowed this negative thinking to go too far. I determined right then and there that I wasn't going to allow the course of my life to be decided by someone else. For me, rewriting my negative thinking was a matter of diverting from the traditional path to a lifelong career. Instead of trying to gain approval of interviewers and potential colleagues in a standard office setting, I would go off on my own and create my own success based on my perceived strengths and passions.

2. Try new things.
When you develop the "I'll Show You" Mind Frame, it is obviously quite important to know where you're going. The best pursuits in life are those that adhere to and employ your greatest personal strengths. If you're an accountant with a gift for marketing, it's time to figure out how you can put those marketing strengths to work. If you're a computer programmer with a strong ability and passion to write, ask yourself how you can use that to create a happier life for yourself. Everyone has a skill—sometimes two, and sometimes many. The truest path to success is to identify that skill and then build a career around it.

But what if you don't know your skill? What if you aren't sure about your professional passions? The surest way to determine the answers to those questions is to try new things. Take a cooking class. Write a short story. Apply for jobs that don't seem to fit your background ideally. Try as many things as possible.

Once you have determined where your strengths and passions lie, it's time to figure out the careers that will best utilize them. Identify your dream job, in other words. Talk to the people who hold that dream job. Figure out what got them to where they are today. With this information in mind, you can begin developing the detail for your blueprint to success (more on that in chapter two).

3.   Listen to your Belittlers.
Remember when I advised you to ignore *your* negative thoughts? Well, when it comes to the negative things people say to you, I advise the opposite. Do not ignore the negative things people say about you. Embrace them. Learn how to make them your motivation rather than your detriment.

If you want something badly enough, the prospect of just ignoring the Belittlers can seem tremendously compelling. *Someone says you can't do it? Just don't listen to them.* If only the Mind Frame were that simple. Unfortunately, from a psychological perspective, ignoring your Belittlers is the same as acknowledging your own doubt. Those without the courage to stand up and listen to the negative things other people are telling them are often destined to succumb to the damage such negativity can cause. Closing your eyes to something you don't want to see doesn't make that thing go away, after all; it only leads to blindness.

The reason it is important to listen to your

Belittlers runs deeper than that, however. In short your Belittlers can often be your greatest allies without ever really knowing it.

Try this sometime: Sit with your Belittlers. Proudly explain to them that you have a dream. Then, when they begin to point out all the reasons you're taking a heavy risk, listen with an open mind. Why? Because a Belittler has a tendency to try to poke holes in a Believer's plans. They do this because it helps them to feel better about how they do not have such passions of their own. Telling you all the ways your plan might fail is their way of overcoming their own perceived inadequacies.

The important thing to notice here is that the Belittlers are actually *highlighting* your plan's flaws for you. While you've got your head in the clouds as you pursue your dreams, you're likely to be oblivious to the inherent flaws in your plan. Belittlers aren't hindered by such things. They probe for flaws with eyes wide open. So listen to what they tell you. Accept that they might be right about certain things. And then, when you go to revise your blueprint, do so in a way that will render those flaws irrelevant.

Refuse to Accept No for an Answer

I've received a lot of no's in my life, so I can tell you this with all confidence: no's are only as devastating as you allow them to be.

"Refuse to accept no for an answer" is one of the most misunderstood clichés. Most people assume it means to be relentless, to never back down from what you want until you've managed to browbeat the no into a reluctant yes. While I agree a certain sense of relentlessness is important in business and in life, I firmly disagree with the true meaning of this cliché.

Refusing to accept no for an answer is actually a matter of adjusting how you react internally to the word *no*. It means when people tell you "no," you shouldn't accept it mentally. You should not internalize the negative aspect of the no, in other words. Try this: the next time you hear a no, don't ask yourself what you've done wrong; *tell yourself* the person who said "no" doesn't know what he or she is missing.

Whenever I hear a no, I just think, "Well, you're going to miss out on what I have to offer." In my time of building the "I'll Show You" Mind Frame, I have come to understand my brand and what I have to offer. This has led me to realize it's the naysayer's loss, not mine.

So remember, no's will happen. It's how you react to them in your own mind that matters.

4. **Internalize the positive; *use* the negative.**
   Don't shy away from the negativity. Remember, what
   your Belittlers say to and about you can be used as
   the greatest fuel imaginable. When those doubts
   are rendered in a positive way, they can be exactly
   the motivation you need to overcome a particularly
   trying obstacle.
      Truly absorbing the negative message and using
   it as motivation is the surest way to make the "I'll
   Show You" Mind Frame a reality. Often it helps to
   write down the things your Belittlers tell you. Some
   Believers benefit from repeating those doubts on
   a daily basis. Others prefer to keep a written list
   somewhere visible, somewhere they see it on a daily
   basis. Consider taping a list of your Belittlers' doubts
   to your bathroom mirror, for example. Seeing these
   doubts every day has a way of bolstering your drive
   and passion to succeed. It is a daily reminder of the
   things you have yet to accomplish in order to turn
   your Belittlers into Believers.

Once you have addressed the four steps above, you will find
yourself in position to address the final step in the "I'll Show
You" Mind Frame process—a step so important I've dedicated
an entire chapter to it. In chapter two you will learn how to
create your blueprint to success. You will begin setting goals
and determining the steps it will take to get there. You will
create a reasonable timeframe and then stick to it, learn how
to set measurable milestones, and discover how to ensure you
meet them at every turn. We will address the importance of a

contingency plan and the greater importance of just throwing all caution to the wind and taking that first step. In this chapter you have learned how to adjust your mindset for success. In the next chapter, you will learn the tangible steps you will need to make that success a reality.

Through it all, remember to stay positive. Use the negative as fuel for your determination. Take that "I'll Show You" Mind Frame and use it to achieve your dreams.

Set Attainable Goals

Bold, Blueprint, Burnout, Breakdown, Benchmark

My first job could be described as what I like to call *think-less*. In other words it didn't require thought. Didn't require creativity. Didn't require any of the major marketing skills I had learned during my time in college and graduate school. Rather than allowing me to fulfill the dreams and aspirations I had for myself, rather than pushing me to be what I knew I could be, this job required little more than for me to serve as a body to keep my desk occupied.

I was a sales recruiter making just over $37,000 per year, and I wasn't happy. That didn't seem like enough money to afford the lifestyle I thought my MBA had earned me. More importantly, despite the scant pay, the job required me to spend extremely long hours onsite. My life got to where it felt controlled by my career. The final straw was when I realized that no matter how I looked at it, I just didn't have any passion for this line of work. For one thing I couldn't see myself holding this same position in two years, much less five or ten. For another, the only thing this job ever brought me was the safety of a predictable paycheck and a few meager employment benefits. That's no reason to stay in a job, I realized. If I was going to invest that much time and energy into something, it occurred to me that it should at least be something I love to do. I had to figure out a better plan. I had to take action. I had to be Bold.

As a girl I'd never dreamed of becoming a marketing expert. It doesn't exactly rank up there with ballerina or princess in the hallmarks of girlish career aspirations. But by that point in my life, I had kind of stumbled into it as a passion. I was a young MBA, and, having exhausted my patience for long-hour jobs, I decided it was time to see what I could really do with my education. With that in mind, I started to look around, be creative, and research what I could do with my degree. I knew I wanted to end up in something that wasn't traditional; I just didn't know what that something would be.

Upon earning their MBAs, many of my friends and former classmates had gone on to become professors. That sounded appealing to me. And yet I knew if I was going to pursue such a career, I didn't want to follow the traditional path. I've always had something of a trailblazer's sense. So I decided to carve out a different kind of career for myself—one that focused on building clientele in the marketing arena in conjunction with a career in academia, specifically in the online sector. This would be my goal. I had hit a brick wall and burned out on my job. Now I would do whatever it would take to build my career as a marketing expert with a keen focus on marketing consultation and online professorships in marketing. This would be the passion that would drive me for many years to come. I would, in essence, become my greatest case study. All I needed in order to get started on my new dream was a Blueprint designed to help me reach the ultimate goal.

By now, you have spent plenty of time thinking about and

assessing your own dreams. You have faced your Belittlers and begun to think positively. Now it is time to take what you know about yourself and your aspirations and use that information to help formulate a Blueprint to success. In this chapter you will gain the insight and learn about the specific steps necessary for creating a plan that will help you identify attainable goals and work toward achieving them. While every Blueprint is as different as every person, the formula for making them work is always the same.

When creating your Blueprint, consider the following steps:

1. **Identify what you really want to accomplish.**
    One of the primary and most common drags on the path to achievement can be a matter of wanting too much or wanting too many different things. You can't aspire to be a tax advisor, a race car driver, and a legendary philanthropist all at once. Yes, it is possible to have multiple passions. And yes, it is possible for each of those multiple passions to sway you equally. But for your Blueprint to be successful, you must choose a singular path. Nothing stops progress quite like spreading yourself too thin. So before you begin, pick a passion and commit to sticking to it.

Avoid Burnout

The trouble with goals is that it's often difficult to tell the difference between the achievable ones and the unachievable. If you're a great salesperson with no military or scientific experience (and a slight tendency toward motion sickness), it's a much more reasonable goal to see yourself on Wall Street than it is to see yourself researching aboard the international space station. And yet so many of us can't help but imagine that awe-inspiring joy of a spacewalk.

One of the most damaging things we can do in life is to pursue an unreasonable and unattainable goal. Doing so sets us up to fail, and when we do that to ourselves we begin to think negatively, second-guess every decision, and grow to doubt ourselves in everything—even in areas completely unrelated to the goal. It's called Burnout, and it can be incredibly derailing. When you burn out, you don't simply lose all the time and effort you have put toward your unachievable goal; you lose the most important thing in life: belief in yourself.

While it might seem clear that aspiring to be an astronaut when you get sick riding in the backseat of your friend's SUV is a silly aspiration, the unreasonable can be far more subtle. Even if your overarching goal makes sense, there are still plenty of opportunities to build unreasonable steps or unreasonable timeframes into your Blueprint.

For example if you want to be a doctor and you're currently working to finish your bachelor's degree, it would be unreasonable to say that two years from now you will be a doctor. The pursuit of goals just doesn't work like that. There are steps everyone has to take. No matter how much you might aspire, no matter how badly you might want it, and no matter how hard you work, you'll still have to complete those goals in the same timeframe it takes everyone else.

A more reasonable goal is to say, "This year I will finish my bachelor's. Then, during the summer afterward, I will score well enough on my MCATs to get into a good medical school. In medical school I will pursue the path of oncology. To reach that end, I will befriend the specialists in that field." And so on.

Imagine your ultimate goal as if it were a twenty-page paper you had to write in college. If you ever encountered such an assignment, you can probably recall the dread of finding something like that on a syllabus. The class seems interesting, yes, but there's that gigantic assignment looming at the end of the semester. The tendency is to fret about how you'll possibly manage to generate so many pages all at once. As a result the further tendency is to put off the assignment until the day before it's due, then find out the hard way that throwing together a high-quality twenty pages all at once on a subject you've barely researched is next to impossible.

Now, if you look at the goal in a more

reasonable fashion, you recognize that its achievement will require the completion of numerous smaller steps. First tackle the cover page. You only have nineteen pages to go. Next assemble your outline, which will in turn lead to a table of contents. You've already stretched it to five pages. Fill out your subheadings. That expands the page count even further. With your structure in place, you might consider researching and completing three to four pages each week. Before you know it, you're only a month into the semester and you're already done with that gigantic assignment everyone else is dreading.

The point here is that Rome wasn't built in a day. Like that twenty-page paper, it's unreasonable to expect to achieve any major goal in life in one day. You must build your Blueprint toward reasonable goals, and you must make each step measured and equally reasonable. Don't set yourself up with the desire to achieve the goal all at once. Set yourself up with the desire to add one notch to your belt today, this week, this month, this year. Work on the notches. Celebrate your progress. And be reasonable about what you can and can't achieve.

2. **Study the background and qualifications of your goal.**

   When sitting down to craft my Blueprint, the first question I had for myself was: how does a person gain online professorships? The traditional path to professorship seemed pretty well plotted out. But how does a person become not just a subject-matter expert but an online presence as well? More importantly, how would *I* achieve that end? I was a young MBA with very little career experience. I had never been a professor of any kind. How would I bridge the gap between my lack of experience and that ultimate goal?

   Ask yourself similar questions. If you want to be an oceanographer, study the field and determine what kind of education you will need. More importantly study *specific* oceanographers to find out exactly what they did to get to where they are today. If the information isn't readily available, don't be afraid simply to call up and ask a person who occupies your dream job—even if it's within your own company. Even if you aspire to assume your boss' position one day. Ask that person what she had to do to get to her current position. Write down everything you learn. Then begin to lay the groundwork for how you will create your own path.

3. **Ask if you fit the criteria.**

   It could be that achieving your goal will require education you don't currently have. It could be that you don't yet know the people who can help you along the path. It could be that you haven't yet presented yourself to your peers and potential hirers as someone who does in fact meet these criteria.

On that last point, when I first began to pursue my goal of gaining online professorships, I was met with resistance based on my résumé. It wasn't that I didn't have the qualifications to serve in my dream job; it was that I hadn't properly accentuated them for the people who would be considering me for positions. I had spent much of my adult life pursuing a career path steeped in marketing, after all, and now I wanted to enter the field of education. This step required me to retool my résumé, pulling out the skills and qualifications that needed to be highlighted.

The bottom line here is that the people who will help you along the path to your dreams will want to know the value you will bring to them, their organizations, and the job you will ultimately hold. For this reason you must first assess that value in yourself, then make it apparent on your résumé. Once you can see it in writing, you will know where you have deficits. When you know where you have deficits, you will be in a better position to turn them into strengths by way of gaining experience in the subjects and qualifications your goal requires.

4. Build and maintain relationships with the people who can help you.
If your goal is to get a job designing shoes for Nike, you would do well to research as much as you can about Nike's history and the company's current

decision makers. Find out who is in the best position to discover your talents and make the decision to hire you. You would be amazed by how much information you can glean from the Internet. It's likely you will be able to discover your key decision maker's e-mail address or contact number. With that information in hand, you can begin building a relationship with this person.

Remember, like anything valuable in life, business relationships take time. Start slowly. Don't ask for a job right out of the gate. A better approach is to ask for advice. There is nothing less threatening and more flattering than being asked for wisdom. If you reach out to your key decision makers with questions about how you might achieve your dream, they will be much more likely to help you than if you approach them with a resume in your hand (or attached to your e-mail, as it were).

That said, there will come a time when it makes sense to send your decision makers your résumé and work samples. By that point they should already be well aware of who you are and what you can do. When this time comes, don't be afraid to follow up with them. Call when you can, but not too often. Let them know you care deeply about this job. Do what you can to build the relationship and allow it to flourish.

5. **Set the bar where it needs to be.**
   "I'm a lofty goal setter," Rachel Hollis, founder of Chic Events, told me. "Big, crazy, outrageous goals I

don't tell anybody but myself. But at the same time, I have smaller stuff I have to accomplish before we can leave for the night. It's empowering to cross those things off my list."

Rachel provides excellent perspective here. There are times when the bar needs to be high. For all those long-term goals, don't be afraid to set the bar at the top. But if you do, be sure to provide yourself with enough smaller steps that you can see progress and actually accomplish things on a daily basis.

For Kyle Smitley of organic clothing company Barley & Birch, the picture is exactly the opposite. "I have short-term goals, but I don't set lofty long-term goals. And I never set an end goal because that's almost like saying that's going to be the endpoint where you have succeeded and can stop trying."

And what an important point that is. Yes, setting the bar high can be a compelling motivator for some, but sometimes it's best not to have a bar at all. Sometimes visualizing an endpoint with too much detail can lead to a lack of motivation once the endpoint is reached. Business (and life in general) is a constant evolution. Yes, visualize your ultimate success; but at the same time recognize that success is a journey, not a destination.

6. **Make (and take!) the steps.**

Every Blueprint must have clear and identifiable schematics. Once you have identified and begun to research your goal, you may begin creating a detailed, step-by-step plan to follow over the days, weeks, and years to come. Assemble all of the information you have compiled through your research and your relationships with the key decision makers who will help you along the path. Now, based on that information, set your goals in a reasonable fashion. Don't set yourself up for failure by expecting to make too much progress at once. Remember, one notch at a time.

That said, don't do the opposite of trying to do too much at once. Don't be the kind of person who does the research, makes the connections, creates the plan, and then doesn't do anything about it. Far too many people have the tendency not to act on their Blueprints because they're too afraid or too overwhelmed to take that first step. Yes, the first step is the hardest, but once it is behind you, and once you begin checking steps off your list, you'll find that overwhelming initial feeling melting away.

Enjoy that you have completed your first step, but don't enjoy it too much. Once you have accomplished your first task, it's time to move on to the next one. Progress is critical. Don't stop for too long to smell the roses or you'll find yourself wandering off the path. Always keep that in mind.

No One Gets Rich Quick

Get-rich-quick schemes. I absolutely despise these things. In my lifetime I have encountered so many people who claim to have found the answer to something that has been plaguing them. They have been convinced that if they do this one simple thing, they can go from 0 to 100 literally overnight. We'll be rich while working from home. We'll lose 40 pounds in a month just by taking this simple little pill. We'll change our whole lives by attending this two-hour seminar.

It should be quite apparent by now that everything worth doing in life requires hard work and must be achieved in increments. Sure, there are stories of people who get rich literally overnight. The dot-com bubble made plenty of people instantly rich. But that sort of thing is representative of less than a thousandth of one percent of all achievement. For the rest of us, success must be accomplished the hard way. For the rest of us, the goal can only be achieved through careful creation and application of a Blueprint.

7. Craft a contingency plan.

If you have ever been involved with implementing a major overhaul of a company's process—for example, serving as the project manager for the live install of new software—you are already well aware that even the best laid plans have a way of coming unraveled at times. There are just so many variables in life that it is often quite difficult to foresee every potential roadblock standing in your way. Sometimes those roadblocks can be mere annoyances. Sometimes they can render your original Blueprint irrelevant.

So that's why a contingency plan is so important. I never do anything without first plotting a plan A, a plan B, and even a plan C. You have to expect the unexpected in business and in life. So once you have your initial Blueprint in place, plot out at least one more that takes into account every foreseeable disaster. If you can see them coming, you'll be that much more prepared to overcome them when they're here.

Breakdowns Happen

I once made a poor investment in some machines. They were designed to distribute DVDs to customers who would pay with credit cards. They were unmanned versions of Blockbuster—precursors to Netflix and the wildly successful Redbox machines you see outside most grocery stores—and I was absolutely certain they were the wave of the future. Well, while I might have been right about that point, I was completely wrong about whether and how this investment would fit into my life.

I bought two of these machines for $25,000 apiece. To me that seemed like a song because I was certain these things were going to be the best thing ever introduced to the movie-watching public. They would be my cash cows. My low-risk, low-effort, high-reward investment.

What I didn't realize was the sheer amount of marketing and legwork that would have to be done to get these things off the ground. I also didn't realize that Netflix, Redbox, and Blockbuster Express would soon come around to kill fledgling ventures like mine. My investment in those machines was dead in the water almost before I had finished fully formulating my dream. I wound up selling them for about a third of what I had paid for them.

Even with your contingency plans in hand, you're bound to encounter the occasional Breakdown. Setbacks happen—especially when you're pursuing a major life goal. That's just a fact. Often, when the inevitable Breakdown occurs, it is the way you react and recuperate that makes the difference between success or failure.

When something doesn't go right on your plan, don't panic. The first thing to do is to sit down and analyze what got you here. Keep an open and constructive mind frame. What might you have done wrong that could have led to the Breakdown? What did you do right that could have been done slightly differently in order to avoid this situation? Will any of your contingency plans be better suited to helping you get back on track?

Next, with the answers to these important questions, it's important that you learn from your Breakdowns. It's equally important that you stay positive. Everything in life is a learning experience. The more you remind yourself of that, the easier it is to take the good with the bad. The easier it is to take the good with the bad, the easier it is to learn from your mistakes. And the cycle perpetuates itself. So when you encounter a Breakdown, remember to learn from it. Study it, figure out how to overcome it, and never make that mistake again.

In my own venture, because I managed to stay positive, I learned many valuable lessons that would influence my future career path and many of my future goals. I learned how to set up a business; how to market from the grassroots level; how to manage contracts; how to deal with customer relations; how to manage relationships with vendors; how to deal with banking, taxes, and revenues; and a wealth of other things I never would have learned had I not failed to implement a pair of movie rental machines. Further, I learned important life lessons like "never go into business blindly" and "always keep everything you do in line with your vision and passion." Had I concentrated only on the negative aspects of my own personal movie-rental machine Breakdown, those important lessons might have been lost to me.

———

8. Benchmark.

When you're taking on a large life goal that is bound to encompass years of your life, the best way to ensure you remain on the path is to identify and keep Benchmarks for everything you do. Don't just create steps, in other words—create steps with measurable timeframes attached to them.

I like to look at my life and my pursuit of goals in terms of annual quarters. In the fiscal world there are four quarters in a year, often referred to as Q1, Q2, Q3, and Q4. These quarters end on March 31, June 30, September 30, and December 31. Every business, whether it's an upstart or a major corporation, measures its progress and success based on quarterly numbers.

I like to manage my life in the same way. Toward the end of every year, I begin creating a plan for the goals I hope to accomplish in the upcoming year. For instance, this year, one of my primary goals was to write this book. I knew that if I was going to have a book in publication by Q4, I would need to have it ready to go to print by Q3. And if that was the case, I had better get it outlined in Q1 and written in first draft form by the end of Q2. There were many other steps in between each of these major milestones, but that was the general plan for how and when I would meet my Benchmarks.

Now, once I had my Benchmarks set, I would be sure to review the progress on each of them toward the end of each quarter. In mid-February I assessed where I stood with the outline. If I had fallen behind, I would have revamped my short-term goals for Q2. As a general rule, it is a good idea to begin laying the groundwork for your annual goals in Q1. Then, if you work diligently, by the end of Q2 you should be seeing the fruits of your labor beginning to grow.

Whatever format you choose, Benchmarks are essential. Quarterly? Monthly? Biannually? It doesn't matter. What matters is that you establish and track specific milestones that will prove (assuming you are honest with yourself) that you have or have not made progress. If you learn you have made good progress, keep following the Blueprint you have set. If not, it is time to refocus your strategy to better reflect the progress you need to make to reach the next Benchmark.

The Long and the Short of It

Some goals are long term. Some are short term. The same is true of the steps that encompass each goal. For this reason it is important that you assess and assign your goals and steps based on reasonable timeframes in which they might be achieved. Not everyone has the same idea of what qualifies as short term versus long term, but for our purposes here I will provide a few examples of what I view as short-term goals (which might take six months to a year to complete) and a few examples of long-term goals (often called the *three-year plan* or *five-year plan*).

Short-Term Goals:
- Achieve a 3.8 or higher GPA this semester.
- Complete 50 percent of my master's degree coursework.
- Get published in a law journal.
- Book and perform at least ten speaking engagements this year.
- Earn a "local small business of the year" award.
- Get a promotion.

Long-Term Goals:
- Graduate magna cum laude.
- Obtain my MBA.
- Make partner at my firm.
- Become a published author and a recognized presence on the seminar circuit.
- Bring my business to the level of being cash-flow positive.
- Crosstrain into another career path and/or land the job of my dreams.

When you create your own lists of short- and long-term goals, be sure to keep a visual reminder of them nearby. I like to use Excel spreadsheets to break down my various quarterly, annual, and multiannual goals. Write your goals down and stick them on the dashboard of your car. Write them on the palm of your hand every day (don't laugh; it works for some people). Consider creating a PowerPoint presentation about your progress at the end of each year. Having this kind of visual representation of the goals at hand and the progress you have achieved on those goals is an excellent way to ensure you remain on task.

Conclusion

I know we have discussed quite a few things in this chapter, but the most important points to remember are to be honest in your assessment of yourself, research what it will take to position yourself to achieve your goals, and, above all, always keep a positive attitude. Nothing comes easily in life—and far too many people have a tendency to give up just before the miracle is achieved. Even with the most detailed and well-considered Blueprint in hand, you are bound to face some Breakdowns. Sometimes, if you're going to get what you want, you have to endure some uncomfortable things. You have to roll up your sleeves and get dirty once in a while.

In closing, be Bold. Plan thoroughly. Market yourself effectively. Remember to stop and look at the full portion of your glass once in a while. But don't dwell on your past achievements for too long, because there is always progress to be made on the next step.

Find Your Niche

Bombastic, Business-Oriented, Best, Burgeoning, Big/Bigger/Biggest

The word *niche* is discussed a great deal in business books. For me the trouble with the way it's currently used is that it seems to imply—sometimes overtly—that finding one's niche is a matter of seeking out market needs one might exploit. Does the market need skilled labor? Well, if so, that's a niche, and you should do whatever you can to become the go-to provider of skilled labor. At least that's the traditional wisdom.

I see the question of one's niche in a much different light. Finding your niche isn't about researching the market's makeup and the nature of what it wants; it's about figuring out who *you* are and what *you* want. If you determine your strengths and follow your dream, your niche will take care of itself. You won't be some inspired person just trying to fill a hole in the market. You'll be your authentic self, and the market will come to you. There's tremendous power in this shift in thinking. Often it is what separates the successful women entrepreneurs from the ones who wind up packing it in and returning to the old nine-to-five.

So your niche—your dreams, your aspirations, and what you were *meant to do*—is a definition of you, not of the market. The goal here should be to figure out how to define yourself and determine where your strengths and dreams fit into the market, rather than the other way around. The trouble is that things like goals, dreams, and strengths don't always make themselves apparent. They enter into the picture at different times for different people, and for far different reasons.

Take for example Prerna Gupta, CEO of Khush, a company that develops intelligent music applications for mobile phones. Before she found her niche and began creating engaging and wildly successful apps, she had to wander for a while. She grew up in a small town in Oklahoma, the oldest child of immigrants from India. She believes the challenges she faced growing up with a different religion and as a different race than most people in her home state helped to shape her character. Where many might become jaded or introverted in the face of such things, Prerna got stronger in her Beliefs and developed a tremendous level of confidence.

"Because I was required at such a young age to adapt to being different," she told me, "it gave me the strength to be an entrepreneur."

According to Prerna, being among the minority during her upbringing made her understand that it's okay to be different. "My thinking was, I have this awesome new idea no one has thought of yet, and everyone thinks it's crazy. I'm going to go out and do it." To follow the old cliché, Prerna learned early on how to dare to be different. As she would find out a few years later, that nature of being different represents the very definition of finding one's niche.

Her first trailblazing effort was to apply to Stanford, the

school that had long been her dream. This proved difficult for a girl from a small town and a public school, but, with a lot of hard work and perseverance, she was admitted. Upon graduation with her degree in economics, Prerna tried to force herself into a job in management consulting.

"It was only about six months before I started to get restless," she said. "I knew at that stage I wanted to start my own business. I felt that staying in a consulting role wasn't going to work for me." She'd had her entrepreneurial dreams prior to this moment, of course, but that had always been part of her ten-year plan. Her niche had different ideas. "Starting a business ten years down the road felt inefficient to me."

As Prerna shared with me, it's amazing how different life can be from what you imagine. Seeking out a niche is a matter of trying to shape your life into what you believe it needs to be. When you do that, you are bound to face occasional failures. Sometimes those failures can be devastating. But if you concentrate on determining *your* dreams rather than on what your dreams are *supposed to be* or how the market tells you to operate, then your niche will form around you. You won't have to force yourself into your area of study. You won't have to research what the market calls for and then try to position yourself to meet those needs. You won't have to suffer through a job you hate and spend all your time working hard so you can advance. You will live your dream, and the market for your services will come to you because of it.

Consider Juliette Brindak, the twenty-three-year-old cofounder of Miss O and Friends, a web community that offers preteen girls a place to socialize, create, exchange ideas, learn, and play together in a safe, nonjudgmental setting. Today, Juliette runs Miss O and Friends and Miss O Moms (the co-view site), which has more than 35 million monthly unique visitors and 1 billion monthly impressions, and are both ranked in the top 100 sites in the world according to Quantcast. Juliette is the embodiment of what it means to allow your niche to form around you rather than actively seeking to fill a market need. For her it just happened that the niche formed at a very young age.

The idea for Miss O and Friends came about organically. As the story goes, Juliette was ten years old and sitting in the backseat of the family car as they returned from vacation. To pass the time, she began doodling a series of female characters she called Cool Girls. The characters were unique, hip young girls free of the usual peer pressure. Naturally, as mothers are wont to do, Juliette's mom saved every drawing her daughter ever did. Later, Mom—a graphic designer by trade—decided the drawings should be brought to life on the computer. There they lived for several years until Juliette had another flash of inspiration.

As a junior high schooler very much faced with the pressures and stresses of being a preteen girl, Juliette wanted to do something empowering for her sister Olivia's eighth birthday. (Incidentally, Olivia is the O in Miss O.) With the help of her mother, Juliette created a series of Cool Girls characters designed after Olivia and her friends. The characters were then printed onto foam-board cutouts and set up for Olivia's birthday party. Juliette, of course, found delight when the girls went crazy for the cartoon versions of themselves, but the more she and her parents dug in to the subject, the more they realized this was something bigger than a memorable birthday surprise. In Juliette's drawings they had found something that tapped into a universal need for preteen girls: representations of their true selves that rise above the petty pressures of young girls' lives.

In her drawings Juliette had found an outlet for the younger version of herself—a place into which she could pour out her stresses by way of creative energy. From her sister's and friends' reactions to those drawings, she realized her need for such a creative sanctuary was universal. "That's when we realized we had something," Juliette said. "That's when we knew our niche had found us."

Too many people don't know their own strengths and how they apply to the market in which they should be operating. Too many others, in search of niches, spread themselves too thin on the things they pursue. This tends to result in a lack of effectiveness—a lack so subtle that many women fail to notice it at all. They spend every day attending jobs they don't truly love. They give far less than 100 percent as a result. Their hearts just aren't into it. They become people who lack motivation and true interest.

Other people fall into the trap of following the traditional wisdom about niches. They look for a perceived need and then try to shape themselves to fit that need. The problem is that some people are square pegs and some holes are round. If you are a square peg and you follow the old wisdom, you simply won't fit your perceived niche. You'll just wind up as one of the many other people following the herd.

Be Honest with Yourself

Many times we see and admire people in business or other avenues—people who are successful in the ways we want to be successful—and we try to emulate them. Those who find their niches are not the kinds of people who copy those who have gone before them. They are the ones who are authentic in everything they do.

When I interviewed the many women who contributed to this book, one of the first commonalities I noticed was how very authentic everyone was. Each woman knew who she was and what she wanted. They all recognized, of course, that they had not yet achieved all of their dreams, but they had pretty good ideas of the qualities they possessed that would help them get there. What separates them from the also-rans in business is that they are able to sit down and say, "This is what I know I'm good at. How can I create a business or harness an opportunity or advance myself based on this strength?" They don't go searching for angles to exploit; they figure out what they bring to the table and then work on ways to maximize those values.

Everyone dreams. Those who achieve their dreams are the people most capable of being honest with themselves. As a child I dreamt of owning a hotel, but as I got older I realized owning a hotel didn't interest me enough to do it day to day. I discovered that my niche—my place of greatest interest and ability—was in marketing. I saw that first when I worked as a telemarketer in an attempt to pay my way through college. Where many of my coworkers would follow scripts or try to tell customers what they wanted to hear, I would make my calls as my true, authentic self. People connected to that, it seemed. People liked me to where I didn't have to be fake to succeed. With this knowledge, a new understanding of my own power as a marketer was born.

Your ability to find your niche hinges on your ability to be honest with yourself. Not everyone comes to the realization of what they need to be by chance. Some must work at uncovering that knowledge. When you are conducting your own search into yourself and your niche, just remember it isn't the market that matters. It isn't even the product or service you plan to sell that matters. People don't choose to do business with you because of the quality of your product or service. They choose to do business with you because of *you*.

So learn who you are. Learn how to maximize that value. And do your part to advertise that value with everything you do and say. Do this and your niche will come to you naturally.

How to Find Your Niche

Remember, the key to this rule is that the search goes inward, not out. It doesn't matter what the market is telling you it wants. All that matters is that you address the market as your authentic self. If you can figure out how to speak, live, and act in genuine fashion, the market will create a niche *for you*.

As you search for your own unique niche, consider the following steps:

1. **Identify Your Strengths**

   It seems a given that the first and most important step to uncovering your niche is to figure out what it is at which you excel. You have to identify your strengths. But how can you do that honestly? It's so easy to tell yourself you're good at something even when the evidence suggests otherwise. Our egos compel us to point the finger in the other direction. "I'm not bad at this. My audience just misunderstands me." At least that's how the flawed logic tends to go. But for the purposes of finding your niche, we must avoid that tendency of ego.

   Honestly assessing your strengths begins with a remembrance of your childhood. Ignore what you think you know about your skills at present. Think back to the skills you possessed as a child. Everything qualifies. If you were a compelling cartoonist like Juliette Brindak, that's important to note. If you thoroughly enjoyed writing stories, that point has value. If you dressed in odd fashions that inspired your classmates to follow suit, there's something to be found there. If you were such a skilled talker that you were often punished for disrupting class, you have a gift that could serve you well today. These were all things at which you once excelled. Most likely they are all things your upbringing, culture, or society eventually weeded out of you. These creative forces helped define who you were as a child—and even if they have been stifled for many years, they still define a part of who you are today.

Don't laugh them off. These skills could be the keys to unlocking your niche. They are your truest and greatest strengths, the path to your most authentic self. They are exactly what will make you so compelling to the market, whatever that market happens to be. Sometimes these strengths come naturally. Sometimes they must be developed with practice over a concentrated number of weeks, months, or even years. But always there is a spark of them evident in our own thoughts and actions. If it compels you, it is a part of you. And if it is a part of you, it is a part of your eventual niche.

2. Avoid the Herd

I mentioned this point in the introduction to this chapter, but it bears repeating here. The trouble with the traditional wisdom about niche finding is that it tries to fit everyone, regardless of personality, strengths, and weaknesses, into a perceived market need. Following this old dictum creates a herd mentality. When one person finds success doing something, everyone in search of a niche tries to follow. This is exactly why everyone in my particular industry is trying to be a life coach these days. A few key people have found success in that arena, and now it's all anyone wants to do.

Remember the lessons of the twelve women I interviewed for this book. Prerna Gupta didn't try to conceive the next Angry Birds; she created an app that appealed to her own personal and highly unique tastes. To her company's great delight, millions of smartphone users shared that taste.

Think beyond the Facebooks and Googles of the world as well. If you look across the landscape of literally every industry, the people you find at the top of the world are there for a reason. They didn't get to where they are today because they're brilliant or because they're lucky, though they often are; they got there because they're genuine and authentic, and always did things their own way. You rarely read a CEO biography that's boring. Rarely do you find a run-of-the-mill billionaire. You only find strong, authentic personalities. It is these very personalities—these very understandings of themselves—that propelled these people to greatness.

The takeaway message here is simple: if everyone's doing it, what makes you unique? Women who make above-average incomes are almost always the ones who dare to be different. They're the ones who listen to the trends and then figure out ways to do something different. While everyone walks in one direction, they walk in another.

So what is that direction for you? By now you should have run an assessment of self that has led you to a better understanding of what strengths you possess. If you listen to the trends, you will be in a position to see in which direction the herd is headed. Once you have seen that direction, you will know where your truest path lies.

———

Don't Be a Jack-of-All-Trades and a Master of Nothing

Some people—whether in search of their niches or otherwise—spread themselves too thin on their aspirations. They'll want to be programmers and marketers and salespeople and politicians all at once. They'll want to wear every hat they can possibly get their hands on. They'll claim expertise at literally anything their colleagues or prospective customers could ask for.

These are rarely the successful people among us. Those who succeed are those who identify their strengths early, realize a craft that fits those strengths, focus on that craft, and invest all their time and energy on honing it. If you have too many irons in too many fires, how can you possibly give the 110 percent required to become good at any one thing? Remember, the market isn't looking for someone who is kind of okay at a dozen things; it's looking for that one person who's better than all the competition at one given thing.

Now please don't mistake me here. I'm not suggesting you can't or shouldn't aspire to possess more than one skill. Having multiple skills is fine as long as they fall under the same umbrella. What I'm advocating is avoiding the common tendency to concentrate on too many things that are unrelated.

There's no such thing as an effective jack-of-all-trades because you can't become what you're meant to become if you're not focused on it. We women tend to be effective multitaskers, but sometimes that ability can be taken too far. We try to be excellent at our jobs and excellent mothers and excellent party planners and excellent homemakers and on and on. We often focus on five or six different things at once, rarely pouring all of ourselves into that thing that makes us special.

As a woman in business, to find your niche you must narrow your focus down to that one thing at which you excel. This is the only way to succeed as an entrepreneur or businesswoman.

3. **Put a Different Spin on Your own Skills**
Sometimes being different is simply a matter of presentation. There are many women who can draw and many women who can design software and many

women with the skills necessary to lead successful organizations. What separates the successful from those who struggle sometimes comes down to that different spin on the same skills.

As a rule, when talking yourself up in any circumstance—whether in business conversation, corporate correspondence, a press release, or a job application or résumé—be as Bombastic as possible. Use words that highlight you appropriately. You're not simply good at something. "I have five years' experience in marketing" doesn't stand out as a descriptor or a compelling reason to use your services. You're the "expert." You're the "extraordinaire."

Be creative with your wording. Catch the eyes and ears of the people you're trying to attract. Whether you're applying for a job or pitching a proposal to a client, you have to show them who you are up front, and you have to do it boldly.

4. Listen to Yourself

In life as well as in business, we're all bound to encounter people who will try to tell us what we should or shouldn't be doing. Many times people have specific ideas of what our skills are. Sometimes they will even go so far as to advise us of what our businesses or innovations should be. As a final step for finding your niche, remember that no one's opinion matters nearly as much as your own.

Many people fail to listen to themselves. They will weigh the opinions of others more heavily under the notion that other people's opinions are less biased than our own. That idea could not be further from the truth, particularly when it comes to business. Most of the time in business, the people you talk to have unspoken motives. They either want something from you or want to sell you something. For this reason their opinions cannot possibly be trusted. This point hints at why it is so important to build the right network. We'll get into that later, but for now remember that if you can be honest with yourself, you are the only person who can tell you what you should or shouldn't be doing. Everyone else will simply try to foist their views onto you or even draw you back into the traditional mind space.

Recall the lesson about the people who have reached the tops of their industries. They all got there—almost without exception—because they refused to dance to someone else's tune. They carved their own paths and followed their own Beliefs unabashedly. The result was the kind of authenticity and commitment it takes to excel in business and in life. These people were not afraid to be different. They weren't afraid to be themselves. They understood the power of themselves. In the coming chapter you will learn how to maximize the power of you. But for now remember to always be different. Be you. Don't find your niche; be your niche.

Understand the Power of You

Brand, Believable, Bragging, Brilliant, Beneficial

"You aren't going to build a brand by sitting behind a computer all day."

Those were the wise words shared with me by Erica Diamond, success coach, award-winning entrepreneur, author, speaker, radio personality, and editor-in-chief of Women on the Fence, a dynamic blog that aims to teach, inspire, and unite women everywhere. At the time of this writing, Erica aspires to expand her blog's brand presence into additional media avenues, but at present she's also enjoying the remarkable success of WomenOnTheFence.com. If she hopes to deliver Women on the Fence to the small screen (her stated goal), I can certainly attest to the fact that she's doing it the right way.

When speaking with Erica, you can hear the energy and commitment in her voice. You can sense she understands her own power as an insightful and driven woman. You can feel how dedicated she is to achieving her dreams. Because of these factors, it should come as no surprise that Erica's brand and her company's brand are so strong. She believes in what she's doing. She has found her niche and connected with a passionate audience. The sky is the limit from here. But, as Erica's opening statement teaches us, passion isn't enough when it comes to brand development. You also have to put in the legwork.

"I remember that Alec Baldwin line from *Glengarry Glen Ross*," she told me. "'ABC: Always Be Closing.'" For Erica, the motto is a little different. "Mine is 'ABT: Always Be Talking.'" No matter where she is or what she is doing, Erica looks for opportunities to strike up conversations. It doesn't matter what the conversation is about—business or otherwise—and it doesn't matter where she is. In a meeting or out to dinner with her husband, she lives by the dictum to Always Be Talking. This helps her to connect with people who might fit into her network, but it also delivers brand awareness by its very nature. How can people know what your business stands for if you don't communicate that message, after all? And what's cheaper and more effective than simply talking? There is no better way than word of mouth when it comes to growing brand awareness.

The Women on the Fence brand is about reaching out to the modern woman who *gets it*—the woman who wants to stop living on the fence and start living her best life. The Erica Diamond brand, meanwhile, is about ignoring the Joneses and chasing your own unique dreams.

"There's really only one you in this world," Erica told me. "When we try to keep up with the competition, we tend to compare our very worst to everyone else's very best. That becomes a spirit-crusher and a nightmare for any dreamer." You have to remember, as we learned in chapter three, that there's only one you out there. That's differentiation built in right there. And the more of your unique qualities you can build into your brand, the better off your brand will be.

"Everyone was opening up a business just like mine in their basement," Erica revealed. "They were all penny pinching so they could deliver the best price. But my business grew because of me. People came to me for my services because of who I was and the ideas I came up with. It's all about the entrepreneur. You're selling the brand of you."

A brand must always come from the heart. It must define who you are. If it's inauthentic, it will never get off the ground. The Dr. Kay brand is about being bold. It's about marketing, about presenting your best self. It's about motivation and inspiration. It's overwhelmingly positive and remarkably empowering. It's progressive. Intelligent. Brash. Market-oriented. Genuine. It promotes the enhancement of women in business. My brand is me, and I am my brand.

For these reasons it should come as no shock that the most important information you can possess when it comes time to begin defining your brand is that information we've spent three chapters assembling: that knowledge of who you are and what you stand for. You have seen already the importance of being honest with yourself, so I won't have to go in depth on the subject here. Just know that nothing kills a brand quite like stretched truths. The brands that succeed are the ones that are unique, but they're also the ones that are authentic.

Need proof? Think about any time a major company's rebranding effort has failed. You don't have to go far to find an example. It happens all the time. A major corporation like Gap or Starbucks does something to change their brand in a way that doesn't fit who they are. The result is a backlash from the consumer base and a poor quarter or two. Brands work the same way whether big or small. Your brand will only succeed if it represents the true picture of you. And it will only soar if you do as Erica Diamond suggests and promote it wherever you can.

How to Develop Your Brand

A brand is the power of you on paper, in person, on the airwaves, or onscreen. It is the extension of yourself that your marketing materials try to project. Because it is representing you, it must also differentiate you. But again, remember that all differentiation must come from an authentic place. We cannot be in the business of inventing strengths and differences. There is nothing else like the Dr. Kay brand, but not because I spent time puffing up the components. There is nothing like the Dr. Kay brand because there is no one like Dr. Kay. And there is no one like you either.

Your brand is a direct representation of you as well as your promise about what you will deliver to your customers or clients. You can't achieve if you're not in tune with what you have to offer. With that in mind, let's examine a few key insights into how to develop a brand that is true to you and your aim.

1. **Determine your vision and your purpose.**
   Ask yourself one question: "What is my business really about?" And don't say it's about making money. If you're going to run a successful company, money really has to be a secondary or even tertiary consideration. The goal of successful entrepreneurs is almost always to make something happen first

and foremost. The money just follows naturally. So what is it that you want to make happen? Answer that question honestly and thoroughly, then write it down in the fewest number of words possible.

2. **Build the right network.**

   Rule #8 goes into this subject in great detail, so I will merely mention it here. The point to take away from this segment is that not everyone belongs in your network. Some people can't help you. Some people won't deliver what they promise. Others are just clutter for your contacts list. So build your network, but make sure everyone who stays in it is *right* for you and for your business.

3. **Conduct a SWOT analysis.**

   Ah, there's nothing quite like a good old-fashioned SWOT analysis to determine the strengths and weaknesses of a brand. For those not familiar, a SWOT analysis is a method often attributed to strategic planning that calls for the analyzer to evaluate the strengths, weaknesses, opportunities, and threats involved in a business venture, project, or, in this case, brand. With a SWOT analysis, you can create a detailed and honest assessment of where your brand soars and where it suffers. You can also find key avenues through which you might grow that brand, and of course determine potential threats to your brand awareness and uniqueness.

4. **Determine your target market.**
   It astonishes me how many entrepreneurs try to build their brands without considering their audiences. The Lexus brand plays pretty well to people with money, but it's not going to fly as far in poor neighborhoods. Something similar can be said about literally any brand in America. Your brand might play better to women than men, to young more than old, to casual rather than formal. So don't build your brand image until you're fully aware of whom exactly it is you want to reach. Once you know that answer, find an authentic portion of yourself that will relate to that target market and emphasize it in your brand accordingly.

5. **Determine who your competition is.**
   Sometimes the best answers to brand questions can be found out in the field. Often, if you're stuck on what your brand should be, the best medicine is to study what the competition is doing. Something specific about their brand might help you to shape yours. Maybe you perceive a shortfall on the part of the competition's brand—one that will fit nicely into the brand you're trying to create. That is certainly something on which to capitalize. Maybe from your survey into your target market, you have determined a flaw in something the competition is doing. Again, that is something that you can use to your competitive advantage.

6. **Remember the Three C's for branding.**
The Three C's for branding are clarity, consistency, and constancy. Clarity should be self-explanatory. You want your brand image, purpose, and message to be unassailably clear. When people see, think about, or learn about your brand, you want them to know immediately and exactly what you stand for. Consistency is a matter of keeping the message uniform. You can't present your brand in print differently from how you present it in person or on the radio or television. This might seem like a given, but so many entrepreneurs are lax on their brand consistency, and few things kill a brand quicker.

Constancy is a matter of getting the message out there to the point where it is almost ubiquitous. That doesn't mean flooding the airwaves or print media with advertisements. It means careful consideration of how to position your brand to where it can have the most lasting impact.

The Online Presence

People often ask me how I have managed to build a brand so strong in the Three C's. One of the first things I always tell them is that a consistent and powerful online presence is key. I did not create such a positive response for my brand and my business without paying careful attention to how I'm received and viewed online.

These days, any discussion about online presence starts and ends with social networking. I have built up substantial followings on Twitter and Facebook because I offer something with which people can identify. I am authentic, I am honest, I am direct, and I am unique. These are the things that drive followers to your Twitter handle or Facebook page.

Of course it also helps to optimize your search engine results. Someone once said, "If you can't Google yourself, you don't exist." If you're not even on the first page of a Google search for keywords that describe your business or brand, how can you expect to reach people? It might cost a little money to optimize your search presence, but every dime is well spent if it helps you reach your potential customers.

So a strong online presence is simple. Build your website according to the Three C's. Optimize that website on search engines. Then keep your brand consistent and powerful across the landscapes of Facebook, LinkedIn, Twitter, YouTube, Instagram, and whatever other social networking sites you can access. Your online brand is what people think of you when you're not there. Make sure they're always thinking the right thoughts.

7. **Conduct a brand assessment**

   Once you have established your brand and allowed
   it to live in the market for a quarter or so, it is time
   to run a brand assessment. How do you do that?
   Simple. Ask twenty of your customers to name one
   word they would use to describe your brand. If your
   twenty responses all come back different, you need
   to work on your consistency. If the large majority
   of them don't meet the message you were hoping to
   send, then your clarity needs improvement.

   It's important that you conduct this survey with
   people who have stakes as customers of your company. Don't ask a partner or employee. You can ask
   a friend, but only if you haven't shared your opinion
   about your brand with this friend before. You want
   people who are interested in your company but do
   not have any insiders' knowledge. These are the kind
   of people who can offer you the honest and insightful
   answers you need.

8. **Deliver your authentic self.**

   This might seem like a repeat of the first tip, but it's
   an incredibly important point to reiterate. Tai Beauchamp, a beauty journalist, an editor, and a truly
   dynamic entrepreneur, lives and breathes this advice
   on a daily basis. When building brand awareness,
   you must deliver what she calls your authentic self.

   "There is only one you," she explains. "That brand

lives in you. So bringing it out is a matter of pouring yourself onto the page."

To see how it's done, look no further than the homepage of Tai's website (http://taibeauchamp. com). On this page she reveals her brand like so:

Tai Beauchamp
pronounced [tahy] [bo-schomp]:
proper noun:

1. Style and lifestyle expert.
2. On-air personality.
3. Entrepreneur.
4. Spokesperson and brand ambassador.
5. Motivational speaker.
6. Content creator. Writer. Editor. Producer.
7. Humanitarian.

idioms:
1. Unapologetic lover of sky-high heels, lashes, blush, and humankind.
2. Believer in the power of women to do it all and look and feel stunning in the process.
3. Style maker helping women make powerful style statements.

Welcome to Tai-land...it's a beauty-full life!

Now *that* is how you make your brand clear and meaningful. You can see on every line how Tai has crafted her brand, and you can sense Tai's purpose, mission, and passion with every point. Most importantly there is nothing about this brand presentation that seems inauthentic. This is the true version of Tai presented on a single page, and it makes an incredibly compelling argument for her services.

<center>~~~~~</center>

Swag

Some people are afraid of swag—all that free and branded stuff an entrepreneur might give to prospective customers or clients. Don't be. While some might roll their eyes at the thought of a T-shirt with their logo on it, nothing promotes brand awareness quite like a walking billboard. And, believe it or not, people are always grateful for the free stuff even if they don't seem to be at first.

In my time of building my brand, I have promoted my company on business cards, T-shirts, tank tops, hats, drink koozies, mugs, key rings, jump drives, gift bags, and anything else onto which I could squeeze my name. The important point was that I kept the brand consistent and engaging. My materials weren't cheesy, and they always delivered the right message. More often than not, they also accompanied one of my presentations, teleconferences, or speaking engagements. They were the free gear up

front, and then the reminders of my brand
presence later.

⎯⎯⎯

9. **Understand your value.**
   There is only one you. That has value, and that has
   power—but only if you know what your personal
   value and power *are*. What do you bring to the table
   that no one else can? Why would someone want
   to invest in you and your company? What makes
   you different from everyone else? These are all
   questions with answers that belong in your brand
   consideration.

10. **Define your positioning strategy.**
    A positioning strategy is, in a nutshell, the way you
    want to be viewed by your customers. When your
    customers think about your brand, what kinds of
    thoughts do you want them to have? When you
    have the answer to that question in mind, you're
    in the position to craft a brand that will reach your
    target market effectively. Remember, however, that
    it's important to conduct a brand assessment every
    quarter to ensure your message is being delivered
    and received properly.

If you want to see the power of an authentic brand that
adheres to the Three C's, just ask Dina Marto of Twelve Music
Group how much her brand helped her career and eventual
business. Dina has spent her career in public relations, A&R,

and music publishing, but like all women in that industry, she had to start at the bottom and work her way up. The day she realized she had a future in the business was when she received a call from industry pioneer Antonio "L.A." Reid.

Dina had met Reid at an event when she was twenty years old. The two had talked for a time, and Dina had felt like she'd made an impression on the music titan, but a long while passed before she heard from him again. She spent the next year trying to make a name for herself in the industry, trying to promote her brand and her presence in the music world, when she got a call from the vice president at Island Def Jam Records, a company Reid had just founded. On the call she learned she was being asked to come in for an interview.

"Little did I know when I sat down at the meeting that L.A. Reid had called the meeting himself," she said. "He hadn't talked to me in a year, but he had filed me away and called me when he needed me. I found that fascinating."

When I asked her why she thought she had lingered in Reid's mind for a full year, she didn't hesitate to single out her brand as the primary link to what would become a successful career path in what remains largely a man's industry. So what is her brand? It's authentic. She clearly demonstrates in person, in advertising, and on her website that she is hard-working, honest, enthusiastic, genuine, and trustworthy, and has tremendous potential.

"If I'm not all the way there," she said, "people can see where I'm going." She is kind, strong, aggressive, and smart—the kind of person who, when you meet her, you just know is going to succeed at whatever she does.

So if you take away anything from this chapter on branding, make it this: Don't attempt to build your brand like anyone else. Be authentic. If you can be open and honest with yourself about your personal value, you won't need to fudge facts on your brand. Focus on your passions. Determine what you're inherently good at, what value you bring to the table, and how you can make an impact in your chosen market.

Dress for the Career You Want, Not the One You Have

Beautiful, Becoming, Blooming, Boss, Brisk

Rule #5 is a quick one because the concept is simple. If you want a job you don't have, you must dress for that job. But before you pass over this chapter's advice, let me just say that it goes deeper than that. Dressing for the job you want and not the one you have isn't a matter of putting on new clothes. It's a matter of internalizing your goals and dreams. If you want to be a lawyer, you can't just dream about being a lawyer and expect it to happen. You have to *live your life* like an aspiring and soon-to-be lawyer.

Internalizing your goals is just like studying in school. You might do well on an exam when you memorize the material, but you won't retain the knowledge unless you internalize it. You don't want only to be able to recall it and say it; you want to make it a part of you. So this rule is about being prepared always to look and act the part of what you really want to become. That means dressing, talking, behaving, and crafting a résumé and, as we learned in Rule #4, a brand image consistent with your ultimate aspirations.

Kanini Mutooni suggests that internalizing your goals is

paramount to success. She lives that advice on a daily basis. When she first began the nine-to-five career that preceded her foray into creating micro-lending businesses, she started by visualizing her goal of becoming a board-level executive within three years. Three years later that was exactly what happened.

"With planning and goal setting, you have to visualize first," she explained. "But you also have to write things down." As Kanini revealed, the difference between just writing goals out and truly internalizing them is to make sure those goals aren't too broad.

"You have to break the goals down into small bits," she told me. "You can never say simply, 'I want to be a millionaire.' That's never the goal. If I want to set up a business and make a half million in a year, I write that down in my journal, then break it down into small steps that demonstrate exactly how I'm going to get there."

As this rule suggests, internalizing your goals and making them personal starts and ends with dressing for the job you want. Sometimes it can be easy for bright and motivated women to begin to feel entitled to success. We begin to think we're so brilliant we don't have to go the extra mile to get noticed. But that is simply not true. You have to be the whole package if you're going to get where you want to go.

Living and dressing for the job you want is so important because success requires everything about what you're doing to be congruent with and reflective of your true self and your aspirations. So much of the time, the way you're presenting yourself is what matters most. If you want to be an entrepreneur, you have to align the way you look with that concept. If you want to be a doctor, the first step is to put your physical appearance and your mindset in line with that goal. When you dress for the job you want, you embody everything about that particular job. You internalize it. Instead of dreaming about maybe becoming something or someone one day, you literally *become* what you are destined to become.

This leads to a large number of incredible benefits. Opportunities begin to spring up where before there were none. People take you more seriously when you tell them about your goals and intentions. You're accepted into the social and professional circles that will help propel you toward your dreams. You make connections, you take action, and, most importantly, you make real and measurable progress every day.

How to Internalize Your Dreams

So now that we've established the power of truly internalizing, living, and dressing the part of what you hope to become, let's consider a few strategies for how to make it happen.

1. **Repeat your dreams to yourself.**
    And do it over and over. Do it until your face turns blue. Do it until you get tired of hearing it. Consider Kanini Mutooni's strategy of writing everything down and breaking it into smaller and smaller pieces. Consider also the idea of pasting those lists in many visible places throughout your home and office. Remember, it's just like taking a test. Whatever worked for you when you were studying for finals, that's what will work for you when it comes time to internalize your dreams. Don't just memorize the thought; absorb it and make it a part of you.

2. **Read, read, read.**
   Continuing with the studying theme, you're not going to get anywhere unless you know as much as possible about the role or job you want to fill or the business you want to start. Thanks to the Internet, there is no shortage of information on any given career or business path. Read about your dreams as often as you can.

3. **Go to seminars.**
   Seminars are such powerful things, especially in a time when most people are content to connect merely online. At a seminar you learn new things, get new insights, develop new ideas, and, more importantly, meet new people. Many of these people are serving in the job or market of your dreams. Meeting them—actually looking them in the eyes, shaking their hands, and making personal connections—is one of the surest ways to determine *how* to get to your dream. They've already walked that path, after all. Who better to explain the specific steps you will need to take?

4. **Discuss your dreams.**
   Sometimes the one thing that separates the dreamers from the doers is accountability. And for many people, accountability only comes from sharing the dream with other people. Letting yourself down is one thing. Letting down everyone you've shared your dream with is entirely another. Knowing there are other people thinking about your goals and

counting on you to succeed is often a tremendously motivating factor.

5. **Dress for your dreams.**
You have already read about the importance of looking the part. Here let's discuss how to determine what the part looks like. First and foremost, always use the industry as a gauge. Look at what the person in your desired role is wearing and doing. Then adapt that wardrobe and those tendencies to your personal style. Remember, we want authenticity, not carbon copies. Use the people in your desired role as a template, not as the final word. Your style and your preferences matter greatly. Be sure to incorporate them in your manner of dressing for the part. The ultimate goal is to be creative and be yourself while also maintaining a level of respect and believability.

Dressing Down

I can't stress enough how important it is to dress for the job you want, so why don't we briefly discuss what happens if you fail to follow this advice? Not dressing for the job you want will lead directly to getting stuck. Why? Because everyone can see as plainly as your face that you're not willing to go the extra mile to achieve your dreams—and that includes you. If you look in the mirror and see the same person you saw yesterday, how can you hope to make any real progress?

Further, the people you speak with in your attempts to advance your goal will not take you as seriously if you're underdressed or inappropriately dressed for the job. When people look to hire you or buy into your business, you want to ensure you present yourself in a way that suggests you've been practicing for ten or fifteen years. If you don't dress in such a way, you look like an amateur, and who wants to pay an amateur when there are professionals out there?

Dressing down suggests you're not a good investment. Poor investments rarely go anywhere—and even if they do, they don't reach the levels to which they aspire. Remember, if you want something badly enough, everything about you has to say, "I am this thing." Without dressing for the part, you don't look like you belong there. You look like an actor in a bad wardrobe.

<hr/>

6. Take action.

By now this piece of advice has become a running theme in this book. There's good reason for this: nothing happens until you take that first step. Don't just say this is what you want to do. Put the wheels in motion. Too often I talk to people with wonderful ideas about what they want to do, but they aren't moving on them.

7. **Find a mentor.**
   The best and most powerful way to internalize your dreams is to interact consistently with someone who lives them. Mentors are so critical in any industry. They are the people in the best positions to tell you what actually *works* when it comes to planning your rise toward your goal. They can help you internalize what you need to internalize because they are literally living your dream.

   When searching for a mentor, the most important thing is to be bold. Don't be afraid to reach out to a high-profile person in the field you want to pursue. Being asked to mentor is a flattering thing, and mentoring itself takes very little effort. Most people jump at the chance.

Interviewing for the Job You Want

Contrary to what you might believe, 80 percent of the reason anyone gets hired is based on their personality while they're in the interview room. Sure, credentials and education matter—they're the things that get you in the door in the first place—but it is who you are and what you stand for that will keep the door open.

In the interview room, you have to come across as likable. The hirer has to buy into your brand. And the only way to do that is to be yourself. Don't be inauthentic.

Next you have to be relatable. That means having things in common with your interviewer. The best way to determine those things, other than conversing naturally and identifying them off the cuff, is to do some research. Before you ever set foot in that interview room, you have to know and understand the company to which you're applying. Know all you can about what the company does, what it represents, what its brand is all about, and where you see yourself fitting in and helping advance the cause. It also helps if you can determine who specifically will be conducting your interview and do research on him or her. Check his or her social media presence. Read any articles that might be available. Inquire of friends or contacts who might know or have worked with him or her. Know your commonalities before you enter the room and you will be more than a step ahead of your competition.

Finally, confidence is key. Wrapping it all together, that confidence starts with the way you dress. When we're dressed well, it tends to manifest in our actions and words. This leads to not only an appearance of expertise but a demonstration of it as well.

8. **Volunteer wherever possible.**
   Sometimes the fields we hope to crack are crowded.
   Often the thing that separates the doers from the
   dreamers is a matter of who is willing to work for
   free. As you will see again and again in this book,
   money should be a secondary concern. If you truly
   want something, you shouldn't worry about what
   you'll get paid in the early going. Take internships.
   Volunteer for efforts related to the company or job
   you want to pursue. Do whatever it takes to experience what it is like to work in the role you want to
   achieve.

   When you internalize something, it means you believe in it
absolutely and pursue it relentlessly. Internalizing a goal means
taking it to bed at night and waking up with it in the morning.
When you truly aspire to something, it's not just a want; it's a
Belief. There are a million aspiring actresses, for example, but 99
percent of them don't reach the goal. That 1 percent who do are
the ones who internalized it—they ate, slept, and breathed the
dream until it became a reality.

   You can have multiple aspirations. You can be flighty with
your dreams. But until you internalize what you truly want,
there will always be a part of you that cannot change to the point
where the dream will become a reality. With competition for
every job as fierce as it has become, those who internalize will
be the ones to succeed.

   I will leave you with one final thought on the subject: How
do you know when you have fully internalized your goals? What

are some of the signs? First you will notice that the people you meet will tell you about the change they have seen in you. Even if it isn't overt, it will become clear through what they say and how they act that they believe in your ability to meet your goals where before they may have just listened to your aspirations politely. Next you will realize that you talk about your goals almost constantly. This is a good thing. The more you talk about what you want, the more likely you are to get it.

The results will come to pass in your career as well. You will get more callbacks from companies that are hiring, prospects, and customers. You will be recruited for the role of your dreams rather than having to apply. You will begin to get feedback from everyone you work with. In the end people will look at you differently. This won't be simply because you have begun to dress for the role you want. It will be because you have *become* the person you want to be.

Reposition, Reinvent, Re-strategize

Bottom Out, Budge, Briefing, Battle-Tested, Bold

Many times, when you get settled into a specific career, things happen that throw you for a loop. Recession. Bankruptcy. Downsizing. Most often these things happen through no fault of your own. The difference between the people who allow these events to overcome them and the people who use them to make themselves stronger is pure determination. The ones who make it through the tough times and come out better in the end are the ones who are determined to find any means necessary to dig out of the hole.

For all of us, when we reach that point where the path we're traveling seems to end, there are four options. We're only going to talk about three of them in this chapter because the fourth one—do nothing and hope things get better on their own—is not an option any of us should want to consider. Conveniently, the other three fit into a nice, repeatable line of words that all begin with the same letter. Say it with me: reposition, reinvent, re-strategize.

Basically each of these three options represents a different level of severity in terms of how one must rethink oneself and one's strategies. Sometimes, when life catches us off-guard, we need only to reposition ourselves. In the world of marketing, *positioning* means putting yourself into the mindset of the consumer. *Repositioning*, then, means assuming a different mindset. When you reposition, you essentially put yourself on a different track toward meeting the same (or a similar) end goal.

Bobbie Kelsey-Grayson, the head women's basketball coach at the University of Wisconsin, once found herself having to reposition for a very different reason. In high school she was a star player on the basketball team. She had never really thought about playing college basketball, but the further along she got in her playing career, the more schools began to take notice. Only when Stanford University came calling did she decide playing basketball at the next level would make sense for her. The day she decided she would commit to Stanford was the day she realized a promising new path had been laid out before her.

Unfortunately the game dealt her a terrible blow in her senior season, causing a severe knee injury that would derail her collegiate career before it even had a chance to begin. With her prospects for playing immediately for Stanford now looking slim, she had two choices: either she could back out of her commitment and move on with a different career path or she could reposition herself as an athlete on the mend. As is the case with most women of strong character and motivation, Bobbie chose the latter. Some people had positioned her as a star in the making, but now, faced with many months of physical rehabilitation, Bobbie had to reposition herself as someone determined to regain the full use of her knee so she could eventually contribute to the team.

Reinventing, meanwhile, means exactly what it sounds like.

These are the times when you come to realize the person you are or the career you are in no longer fits with your future. These are the times when you must reassess who you are and what you are doing, come to terms with the things that aren't working, and completely reinvent yourself.

For Bobbie Kelsey-Grayson, that first occasion of reinventing came as she approached the end of her time at Stanford. She had recovered remarkably well from her knee injury and had become a vital contributor to a tremendously successful team. She had never really considered playing professional basketball, but the more the mobility returned to her knee, the more attainable that goal became. As she approached her senior season, she decided she would go wherever the game took her. But just as that season began, she suffered a second severe knee injury.

"You have to self-examine in times like that," she told me. "You have to look in the mirror and ask yourself what you're willing to do to achieve your dreams."

For Bobbie the answer was to continue with the game she loved so dearly in the only capacity left available to her. She decided to reinvent herself by becoming a coach. She began her path to a head coaching position by way of a series of assistant coaching jobs at stops all across the country, eventually landing back with her alma mater and helping her former team to an unprecedented run of success.

Our final path, *re-strategizing*, means to examine the strategies you have employed on your career path or in your business to see whether they are in need of an overhaul. Many times, when we're faced with difficult circumstances—a firing or a loss of a key customer, for example—it's because the strategies we have been relying on are not quite where they need to be. Often it is difficult to see the flaws in these strategies until after the difficulty makes itself known. Hindsight always offers sharper pictures of the flaws, after all. Those who succeed in the face of these kinds of setbacks are those who are willing and able to examine their strategies honestly, seek advice from their peers, and re-strategize in a way that will allow them to avoid repeating the same mistakes.

As a head coach of a college basketball team, Bobbie now holds her dream job, but she didn't get to this lofty post without having to re-strategize a few times along the way.

"The game of basketball requires you to re-strategize almost constantly," she explained. "It's a lot like a chess match. Every strategy your opponent uses impacts your strategy. If you can't re-strategize, you can't win."

Sometimes re-strategizing is a small matter, like shifting from a man-to-man to a zone defense. Sometimes it's a larger matter, like restructuring your overall game plan following a firing. "When you lose your job," Bobbie told me, "you have to make some tough decisions. You have to find a new position. You have to uproot yourself. You have to sell your house and move. But the most important thing is to re-strategize on what you did at your last job that didn't work."

For Bobbie that new strategy involved calling some former contacts she thought she would never have to work with again, but in the end her new strategy worked far better than the old one ever could have. She encountered a few bumps in the road on her path to her dream job, but now she occupies it proudly. "God taught me to stop saying what I won't do because that just won't work," she said. "You've got to understand there's a plan for everyone. The trick is figuring out how to follow it."

Reposition, reinvent, re-strategize—words to live by. We all must endure tough times in our lives. When something isn't working, our goal must be to figure out something new. The Three R's are a matter of putting a different spin on yourself. When you reposition, you put yourself in another mindset. It's a little like when an artist decides a painting isn't working for her, so she makes a few adjustments on the same canvas. When you re-strategize, it's a matter of going back to the drawing board. It's a little like when an artist gets so frustrated with a painting that she paints a new version over the old. When you reinvent, you have reached a point when repositioning and re-strategizing haven't worked and it's time to create a new version of yourself. This is the point when the artist throws out the original canvas and starts again on a new one.

So with that in mind, let's turn the search inward and see whether it is time for you to consider any of the Three R's.

When It's Time to Reposition…

When it becomes clear the strategy you're using or the career you're occupying isn't working, it's time to reposition. How do you know when this is true? You might be getting negative feedback (or worse, no feedback) from your superiors, peers, or customers. You might have fallen short of expected profits or production. You might feel a lack of personal or professional satisfaction. When any of these factors crop up in your life, it's time to do something different—nothing drastic, mind you, but something different. It's time to put a new spin on what you're already doing, time to make it fresh and new. You're not going back to the drawing board and completely revising your strategy; you're just redirecting it a little.

Take Apple Computers for example. Remember that great advertisement from 1984? The one where the rebellious young woman runs into the brainwashing chamber and throws a sledgehammer through the video screen, freeing all the mindless drones from the tyranny of the speaker? Think about what Apple represented back in the mid-'80s. As the classic advertisement suggested, they were an alternative to traditional computer systems. Their product wasn't flashy, but it certainly got the job done.

Now consider what you know about Apple today. They've dropped *Computers* from their name and, if anything, they have become *all about* style and flash. The functionality and usability remains, but without that repositioning that occurred shortly after Steve Jobs was brought back into the fold, they wouldn't be the global technology titan they've become. Apple's repositioning took them from languishing as the alternative to traditional computers to dominating as the coolest, trendiest, and most innovative brand in the consumer electronics market.

So you know that repositioning is about bringing more flavor to what you already do. You know it's about adding benefits to what you already offer. You know it's about making your strategy, output, or offerings more attractive. But how do you do it? Good question. Consider the following tips:

- **Run a cost benefit analysis.**
  A cost benefit analysis (CBA) is a process by which you compare and contrast the benefits of a project, decision, or strategy with the projected costs. If you can be honest about the perceived benefits and the projected costs of your project/decision/strategy, then running a CBA will help you achieve two things. First you'll have a better idea of whether your project/decision/strategy is a sound one. Second, if

you run a CBA across all of your projects/decisions/ strategies, you will gain a clearer picture of which of them are the most beneficial and effective. A CBA shows you where the money is when compared to the effort—and, more importantly, when compared to the prospective gain you will receive. Be thorough with this analysis and you'll know exactly what is working and not working.

- **Conduct a brand assessment.**
  It's possible your strategy has stalled because you're not projecting the message you had intended. Running a brand assessment is a simple thing. Ask twenty of your customers or coworkers to tell you the one word that describes your brand. If you're not getting back the responses you were hoping for, or if the responses are too variable, then it's time to reposition your brand in a way that better delivers your message.

- **Analyze your features and benefits.**
  Ask yourself this question: "What is it specifically that I bring to the table?" In other words what are some of the things you do more effectively than others? When you know the answer to these questions, ask yourself whether you are applying those features and benefits as transparently as you can. If your employer or your customer isn't seeing all those great things you're bringing to the table, it's time to reposition yourself in such a way that they can. This could mean revising your marketing strategy,

volunteering for more projects at work, or just picking up the phone and making some calls.

- **Analyze your target audience.**
  Think back to Apple again. They weren't quite the technology giant they have become back when they were targeting standard computer users. They took off into the stratosphere only after they shifted focus to young, hip, tech-savvy consumers. It wasn't that their products weren't great. It wasn't that the people working behind the scenes weren't brilliant. It was that they were positioning themselves for the wrong audience. Ask yourself if it's possible that you could be doing the same. If the answer is yes, then return to your market analysis and see if there are any other demographics that might make better sense for you.

- **Revise your marketing plan and strategic approach to the new market.**
  Once you have a new market in mind, compare your features and benefits to the market's needs. Then craft your marketing strategy around demonstrating those features and benefits directly to the new target consumer. As you learned in the chapter on branding, make sure you're getting what you want to accomplish across in one word.

  Consider the story of Kyle Smitley of Barley & Birch, a designer and wholesaler of "unabashedly organic, planet-saving clothes." Kyle has built a remarkable company—one that gives half its profits to charity—from the ground up. She could continue on this line, but she sees her future taking her elsewhere.

"I'm going through a repositioning at the moment," she told me. "We're going to sell Barley & Birch to a company with a similar mission." Her plan from here? "Before, I was always the face of the company. Now I'm shifting focus. I'm at the point now where my identity is not completely tied to one business. I'm looking at expanding from one business into several."

The next stop for Kyle? She hopes to establish an organic ice cream company on the same principles that worked for Barley & Birch. "That's one thing you can rely on when you go through things like repositioning. The new strategy will always work if you hold on to the successful underlying principles."

When It's Time to Re-Strategize...

You know it's time to re-strategize when your original strategy hasn't worked. You may have attempted a repositioning at this point, but that hasn't led to the results you seek. Recall from Rule #2 the importance of benchmarking. Here is where those well-defined benchmarks become valuable. If you're examining your strategy and seeing that every three, six, or nine months you're missing several key benchmarks, something is out of whack about your approach. This is when you know it's time to re-strategize.

So is it time for a new strategy? Then let's consider the following three steps for crafting a good one.

1. **Assess each benchmark from your original blueprint.**

   Determine the progress you have achieved at the three-, six-, and nine-month points of every benchmark in your blueprint. Some benchmarks will have been achieved. Others will have fallen short. It is the latter on which we must focus.

2. **Analyze your steps.**

   In your blueprint you determined a specific course of action you would take to achieve your benchmarks and ultimate goal. That course of action contained a number of steps you would need to take on your journey. Here you should analyze your performance on each individual step. Is there something particular that has caused you problems? Answering this question for each step will help you figure out what's causing your strategy shortfall.

3. **Go back to the drawing board.**

   With your missed benchmarks and your underperforming steps in hand, you now have a clearer picture of where the problems are occurring. This is all you need to define a new strategy—one that deftly avoids the problematic steps or benchmarks. Be honest about where the shortcomings reside. If, for example, you have said you want to open a business within a year, but you're on month nine and you've only gotten as far as completing the paperwork to form an LLC, then you're obviously going to have to devise a strategy that will give you more time or allow for more effort on your part. Keep in mind that re-strategizing won't work if you're not honest with yourself.

When It's Time to Reinvent…

By this point in the spectrum, you've already exhausted the other two options. Repositioning hasn't worked, and no matter how many times you re-strategize you find yourself coming back to square one. Here's where we throw out the old canvas and start working on a whole new one. This is where you scrap the idea or pursuit and start turning the search inward. The question we attempt to answer here is: what is it about *me* that needs to change?

When you think about reinvention, think about Ford. Prior to the economic crisis of 2008, Ford was a declining company with a line of only mildly popular cars. Since their bailout, they have come back as one of the most stable companies in America, complete with a rebranding and a host of attractive and efficient cars that seem to appeal to a broader range of modern Americans. To reach this enviable end, they had to go back to the drawing board and revise how they did almost everything in the company. Instead of simply trying to rebrand, they approached the matter as if the old Ford didn't exist. They came up with a new Ford, developing it from the ground up—and today they reap the tremendous benefits of that decision.

If you reach the point where you feel you must reinvent yourself or your company, consider the following pieces of advice:

- **Forget everything you've done to this point.**
  Trying to hold on to certain strategies that may have

worked for you is the surest way to prevent a rein-vention. Avoid the tendency to want to drift back into new strategy. We're trying to create a new *you*. So start off with the mindset that the old you doesn't exist anymore. Imagine yourself as a kid fresh out of college. Remember the way you felt back then? You were a clean slate, and a world of possibility stood before you. That's how you should think of yourself now. Nothing you have done to this point happened or matters. All that matters is what you will do with the new you.

- **Decide what you want to be.**
  Remember, that thing you want to be can't be the same as it once was. You're a new you. This is a tough reality to grasp because most of us spend so many years dreaming about achieving that one thing. When it doesn't work out, it's tough to let go of the old dream. But here we're coming up with a new you, and that new you must do some soul searching to determine what the best new path might be.

  Your brand doesn't exist anymore. Your old target market is no longer a consideration. Your former blueprints and your benchmarks aren't relevant. New versions of these things will come in time. For now, decide who you want the new you to be.

  Whatever decision you make, be sure to base this new viewpoint on the features and benefits you highlighted during your repositioning. What are the honest strengths you bring to the table? Next consider shaping your strengths into a branding approach you admire. What are the brands you value most? Is there anything about you that matches up with them? These are the things around which to build your new path.

Sometimes Your Passion Reinvents You

Celebrity photographer Drexina Nelson wasn't always the high-profile and wildly talented artist she has become. There was a time when she worked in corporate America—at a leadership development program for the Ford Motor Company, incidentally—but when an injury forced her to take a leave of absence, she found the time to pursue her true passions, which have always been makeup and photography.

"I grew up reading *Vogue*," she confessed. "I always loved that type of thing. So when I had my opportunity, I found my passion and pursued it."

Little did Drexina know that for her the reinvention process was only just beginning. She had gone from being a key contributor to a large corporation to becoming a rising star in the world of photography, but she did not realize how her unique approach to the art form would create a shift in the market for her services.

"My goal wasn't to be a celebrity photographer," Drexina said. "It was to be a great photographer who brought out the inner beauty of people. It's not about whom I shoot. It's about how I shoot them. It's about bringing out who that person is regardless of where they come from."

The lesson Drexina learned from this unexpected turn in her career path was that you always have to follow your passions first. Even if your skills seem trivial to you or your dreams seem too whimsical, every effective reinvention of oneself centers on those passions. Had Drexina stayed with Ford, she might have been successful in a different way, but she likely would not have achieved the same level of happiness she has found in pursuing her passions.

• **Get out and do it.**
With most things in life, the first step is always the toughest. When you reinvent, that first step tends to be even tougher. You are, after all, dispelling everything you've done to this point and doing something completely different. That can be scary. Terrifying even. But don't let your fear cause you to drag your feet. Don't stall. Don't wait. Get out there and take action. If you hope to achieve your new dreams, you

have to jump off the cliff and build the airplane on the way down.

There comes a time in every businessperson's life when one of the Three R's becomes necessary. The important thing to remember is that you're not the first person to have to revise your brand, your strategy, or even yourself. Keep that in mind when it comes time to go back to the drawing board and you will be in better position to make the honest, accurate, and appropriate decisions that will lead to greater success in the future.

Now, with your new position, strategy, or you in hand, it's time to address perhaps the most important rule of all: be relentless in your pursuit.

Be Relentless in Your Pursuit

Bound (and Determined), Ballistic, Belligerent, Bossy, Busy

In interviewing the twelve successful women who contributed their wisdom to this book, a consistent theme began to emerge: success has a direct correlation to a person's unwillingness to give up. In business and in life, we are all destined to encounter our fair share of no's. Even the greatest ideas ever to see the light of day faced at least a few people who could not see their greatness and did not wish to invest the time, energy, and money it would take to make them realities. As an entrepreneur and even as a nine-to-fiver, you can't get where you want to go without encountering a no once in a while.

The difference between those who succeed and those who fail is that the former refuse to allow a no to become a permanent setback. These are the kind of people who are relentless in the pursuit of their goals. When they encounter resistance, problems, setbacks, and outright no's, they do not see them as the endgame. They see them as challenges that must be overcome. Where many would bend or even break at rejection, the successful among us use it as motivation to make themselves and their products or services better.

"Those no's push me forward," Savannah Britt told me. "They are my motivation to achieve future yeses." Even though she is only eighteen, Britt indicated that she is no stranger to the sometimes devastating word. Certainly she has been wildly successful as a magazine publisher—particularly considering how remarkably young she is—but that success did not come without the occasional setback.

Britt's story begins like it does with most child prodigies. By eight years old, she was already a published poet. A year later a New Jersey newspaper called *The Kitchen Table News* began paying her to review children's books. Today she is the youngest magazine publisher in the United States (and was the youngest in the world until recently), and the editor, writer, and chief contributor of GirlPez.com, one of the most popular fashion sites on the web. But she didn't get to her lofty seat without some difficulty. Those who know her recognize that while she might be the youngest magazine publisher in the US, she might also have been one of the youngest people ever to have been fired by a newspaper.

At the age of twelve, with *The Kitchen Table News* folding due to declining readership, Britt found herself without a job. That's the kind of no that would devastate most people—particularly when the person in question is still a young child—but Britt held strong, rebooted her determination, and pressed on. By the incredible age of twelve, she was the proud publisher of a magazine called *Girlpez*, a publication that covered (and continues to cover in its online-only format) major pop culture events like concerts, fashion shows, and celebrity interviews.

Though *Girlpez* has seen great success in the four years

since its inception, Britt has not exactly shed the occasional no's. "Since I'm so young," she said, "some people in the business don't really acknowledge me because they assume I don't know what I'm doing." For many of us, visibility is the primary obstacle to overcome. We need to do things that get us noticed by our employers or considered by our potential customers. We must connect with decision makers or make compelling pitches to investors. Many times there are things about us or our presentations that destine us for a no or two. For Britt the no is practically ever present because of her age. Before she can find success in almost any situation related to her company, she must first overcome the built in no of age discrimination.

But Britt is wired like a determined entrepreneur. Those no's don't become setbacks; they become *motivation*. In this chapter I intend to demonstrate how you can begin to think like Savannah Britt. You're going to face no's as you try to climb up the ladder at work or guide your company, idea, or venture to success. The trick is to turn those negatives into positive reinforcement. The trick is to be relentless.

Never Give Up

When we encounter our first (or second, or third, or fourth…) no, it's so easy to stray from our focus. It's so easy to stop improving yourself and your craft. Drifting back to the status quo, returning to what is expected of you, and retreating into giving up is just so much easier than striving to overcome, changing strategies, and forging ahead.

No has a tendency to create so many distractions. It causes us to lose focus and begin concentrating on things that don't matter. Worse, we begin to make excuses for why it's okay for us to settle for the no. "I guess this just wasn't a good fit for me," we tell ourselves. "If it was meant to be, it would have come more easily." Not so. There's that old cliché that nothing worth doing in life comes easily. In the realm of business and entrepreneurship, those words could not ring truer.

If you are going to succeed in your goals, whether personal or professional, you must work on ways to avoid the mindset that allows you to give up or slow down even for a second. You need to stop looking for reasons to justify the no's and start thinking there is nothing in the world short of a silver bullet that will prevent you from achieving your goals.

Kanini Mutooni achieved this mindset by setting measurable goals for her career at a young age. "Even at sixteen," she told me, "I visualized myself having a degree in accounting in four years. Then I told myself that when I graduated I would work for the cream of the crop in financial consulting." That visualization and determination led to a relentless pursuit of progress up the corporate ladder. After finishing university, she quickly landed a job with Ernst and Young. Two years later she was promoted to a vice president position with Merrill Lynch. Six years later she would be promoted again, then headhunted into the audit director position at a private bank in London. Each promotion fell into the schedule she set for herself, and each was the result of her relentless pursuit of her ultimate goals.

For trainer and business consultant Ana Cortés, overcoming setbacks started off as a rather serial affair. "I've had a lot of no's," she confessed to me. "I've started at least fifteen companies, and each one has suffered setbacks. When I moved from Mexico to Phoenix, I had to close five companies at once."

So what is her secret to overcoming such adversity? "I approach my entrepreneurial endeavors with the mindset that my passion and purpose in life can be achieved in many different ways." With that brand of thinking, even the most crippling no's have little effect. Cortés has seen such success with her training and consulting business—in addition to several other businesses along the way—that she knows she is capable of repeating that kind of success in whatever she chooses to do.

Never giving up isn't easy. It takes a great deal of work. When I was trying to create my presence as an online professor, I would have to stay up late every night conducting research, retooling my strategies, and thinking about ways I could become better at my craft. To aid in my endeavor, I had to make some tough choices and delay some gratification until after I achieved my goals. For instance I didn't find going out to social events particularly useful at that point, so I spent many of my days and nights at home, maintaining my pinpoint focus on finding that first contract with a university.

When you're trying to make a career transition, open a business, or take an existing business to the next level, you truly have to eat, sleep, and breathe that goal. You have to *become* it. You have to be as creative, innovative, and above all relentless as possible. So how do you do that? I'm glad you asked…

1. **Never give less than 110 percent.**
    People say this all the time: if you want to succeed in life, you have to give 110 percent all the time. The problem for most people who truly want to achieve their dreams is not the effort itself. If you really want something, giving it your all and then some is not nearly as tiring as it might seem. Where many people fall short—even the ones who have that burning desire to achieve—is that they don't

know what 110 percent *looks like*. They pass each day assuming they're giving it their all and bettering themselves when in fact there is plenty more they could be doing.

So how do you know if you're giving 110 percent? The first place to look is at your shortfalls. If you're not getting the results you want, you could be working harder. If you ever find yourself stagnating on any one thing related to your goal, you have to do something to break out of the rut. On a personal level, assessing whether you're giving it your all begins with examining the feedback you receive from clients, customers, employers, family, friends, and anyone else willing to give constructive criticism. Beyond that it's a self-correction kind of thing. You have to know internally that you're offering your goals 110 percent. If you're trying to fund a startup, ask yourself if you've really gotten yourself in front of as many potential investors as possible. If you're looking for a job, ask yourself if you might be able to send out more résumés each day. If you're trying for that promotion, ask yourself if there's something more you could be doing to catch the boss's eye.

If you're not giving 110 percent, you won't be seeing the results you expected. You won't be hitting your milestones in the timeframes you set. You won't be getting enough feedback. Think of it like this: Imagine you lost your job during the recent economic recession. If you were like one of the millions of other people in the same situation, you might have spent weeks, months, or even years telling yourself there just aren't any jobs available. If, in your own pursuits, you have ever heard yourself making excuses like this one, you're not even close to giving 110 percent. The 110 percenters who lost their jobs during the recession did whatever they needed to do to secure not just new work but new futures. They opened businesses. They knocked on every door. They went back to school to retrain themselves for the skills they would need to remain employable well into this new age. That is what 110 percent looks like.

So are there any signs to look for that might indicate when you've reached your own 110 percent? Certainly. You'll get positive feedback from many of the people in your life. You'll receive more phone calls than ever before. Your e-mail inbox will light up with missives offering new opportunities (and not just the poorly worded spam that gets swept up by your junk-mail filter either). If you're writing a business plan or an important project at work, you'll see that first page transform to the tenth and then the twentieth. Production—true and measurable results—will seem to appear magically before your eyes.

I have never seen anyone give 110 percent of themselves and not get any results. With hard work, anything can be done.

2. Listen to your Aha Moments.

We've all had Aha Moments before. These are those moments when the solution to a predicament that previously plagued us becomes immediately clear. It's hard to explain where they come from; we just know we feel inspired when they arrive. These are the moments when something in your mind or something in one of your working relationships just *clicks*. Where before there were obstacles, now there are opportunities.

The trouble is that too few people know what to do with these Aha Moments. Some people let them pass by as if they were mere flights of fancy. Inspiration is critical to success in literally any field. Never pass it off as a whim. It is the driving force behind innovation, creation, and ultimately success.

Now, that said, not every Aha Moment needs to be pursued with the aforementioned 110-percent vigor. Some are more related to your primary goal than others. Some motivate you more than others. Some influence you from the background; others resonate loudly.

So what if you don't have the time or the patience to wait around for your next Aha Moment? The process can be sped along. Inspiration can be manufactured by doing creative things, getting out into the world, meeting creative people, and reading inspirational books. My most recent Aha Moment came when I read Barbara Stanny's brilliant *The Secrets of Six Figure Women*. From the moment I put that book down, everything in my life began to make sense. My thinking transformed. Previous obstacles melted away. My 110 percent became that much stronger than it was before.

Do not ignore your Aha Moments. Follow your inspirations. Embrace those clicks, those moments when the lightbulbs come on. These are the times when possibilities make themselves known.

3. **Do your homework.**

I've mentioned this point before, but it bears repeating. Any time you plan to enter into something—whether that's the pursuit of a new job or a new opportunity for your business—you *must* do your homework. Research everything you possibly can before you ever enter the room. Knowledge is, after all, power. More often than not, it is the edge necessary to beating the competition and securing the opportunity.

Once you've done your research, develop your strategy around it. Keep honing that strategy until you can see no flaw—then hone it some more. And when you have everything in place, implement, implement, implement. Do not rest until you feel like you know everything there is to know and until you can actually *see* your strategy in motion.

4. **Eat, sleep, and breathe your craft.**

If you're truly giving 110 percent of your effort, then your craft starts to feel more like a new hobby than a job. One of the questions I asked each of the twelve women I interviewed for this book was, "What are your hobbies?" Not surprisingly almost every one of them struggled to come up with a list. For most of them, hobbies focused almost exclusively on the things that would make them better and stronger at their jobs and lives—reading, jogging, networking, etc.

Now, I'm not suggesting you should close yourself off from the world and become a single-minded person forever. That's no way to go through life. I merely suggest you delay some gratification until you get your plan of action moving and until you have achieved success.

Eating, sleeping, and breathing your craft means taking your next steps and your milestones to bed with you every night, and it means thinking about them the moment you wake up. It means calling prospects constantly. It means taking as many interviews as possible. It means e-mailing résumés every day. It means taking all the steps necessary to get to where you need to be. It means being unconventional in conventional times. If there is ever a moment when you're not thinking about what you need to do next to achieve your goals, you must push through that moment and get back on task.

5. **Go above and beyond the competition.**
When you're eating, sleeping, and breathing your craft, this final step comes naturally. Here you must find ways to do things more efficiently, better, and more creatively than those do with whom you compete. It's all about strategy and timing—with timing often being the key. But, if you've done your homework, operate with inspiration, and give 110 percent

of yourself to the things you want, the competition doesn't have a prayer.

Where many of your peers find success is through their unbending unwillingness to let the word no become a setback. They are at all times relentless. With these five steps, you too can live a life free of stagnation and align yourself with the path of consistent upward movement. Your milestones will pass by more quickly than you could ever imagine. Through your 110-percent effort, you will become more powerful than you ever thought possible. Before you know it, you will have reached your ultimate goal.

But, as is the case with anything in life, you can't reach that end without a little help. Friends, family, and acquaintances can only take you so far. Success in any field depends on the quality of the network you build for yourself. Note that I wrote *quality* and not *size*. Read on to discover why the right network is always better than a large network.

Build the Right Network

Build, Buzz, Blessed, Blissful, Bureaucratic

Networking events. We've all been to them. There was a time in my career when I believed in the conventional wisdom about networking: the more business cards you can collect, the more likely you'll be to succeed. For many professionals the tendency over the past twenty years or so has been to try to build the largest and most diverse network possible. This was the dawn of networking events—big, teeming pools of people just trying to take and give contact information, everyone—even the people who could actually deliver something for those they meet—getting lost in the white noise.

You can already see the problem with the conventional wisdom on the subject. When you go out just trying to meet and keep up with as many people as possible, you wind up with a contacts folder, a LinkedIn page, and a stack of business cards from people who can't truly help you. You're not building a network; you're building a phone book. And if it's a phone book you want, you might as well save yourself the time and effort of going to networking events and just pick up the yellow pages and start dialing.

I understand the philosophy behind the conventional method. You never know who you're going to meet, so the more people you meet, the better your chances of hooking that big fish. But the thing about entrepreneurship or even climbing the corporate ladder is that it takes precision. You need a scalpel with a laser sight. Meanwhile traditional networking is more like the shotgun approach. In these modern times, those of us who are passionate about success need a better strategy than a shotgun can provide.

So let's throw out the conventional wisdom. Instead of devising schedules that allow us to meet an enormous number of people, let's determine a strategy for how to meet and build relationships with the right kind of people. In other words rather than expand your contacts folder, let's figure out how to make each name in that folder more valuable to you, your business, and your ultimate goals. If we can assemble a strategy that works for you, everyone in your network will be able to deliver something you need rather than just claiming they can, only to let you down later; everyone will work in roles that actually benefit the things you want to do; and everyone will be like-minded enough that they share and understand your goals, yet different-minded enough to help you see things in a new light whenever necessary.

What Makes a Contact the *Right* Contact?

Put another way, how can you tell the difference between a contact who can help you and a contact who just claims he or she can? The problem with networking—traditional networking in particular—is that it depends too heavily on strangers actually delivering on the things they tell you they can deliver. The trouble is it's just so easy for some people to stretch the truth when they're speaking with someone they've only just met. If they think the relationship might somehow benefit them, people will tell you anything you want to hear. Some people have become so skilled in the art of overpromising that most of the time their promises seem completely genuine.

The simple answer to the question in this section's header is that when we're talking about genuineness, the best gauge is the results themselves. Don't listen to what this person is telling you he or she can do; examine what he or she has *actually done*. If after a couple of weeks the answer is "nothing" or "not nearly what was promised," then he or she is not a contact worthy of your network. So the proof really is in the pudding. When examining your contact list, ask yourself if what this person says fully aligns with what this person does.

Think of it like a job interview. You're figuratively interviewing everyone in your current network and literally interviewing everyone hoping to join your current network. With job interviews you see this sort of thing all the time: a candidate comes in with a decent résumé and reasonable referrals but then absolutely nails the interview. The hirer gets really excited about this candidate because he or she is so personable on the spot. But then once the candidate becomes an employee, he or she underperforms. This sort of thing happens all the time simply because people are so skilled at riddling out what others want to hear. The trick is to see through the exaggerations and focus solely on the results.

It's like walking into a clothing store and buying a new dress. You pick one out, hand the clerk your money, and expect to get a dress in return. If, after handing over your money, the clerk fails to give you your dress, you're probably not going to return to that store. You might go online and post a bad review for all to see. You might even tell all your friends and family never to patronize that store. It's so easy when we're making a purchase to tell good service from bad service, delivery from non-delivery. Why, then, is it so hard to see it in our contacts list?

The answer is probably *human nature.* Most of us want to believe that the people we're speaking with are being straightforward about everything. Nobody wants to believe they're being lied to. So we give almost everyone we meet the benefit of the doubt—particularly when that person is promising us the big results we've long been pining for. But if we're going to build the right network, we have to see through that typical human nature and look only at the bottom line. When it comes time to deliver, the right contacts always perform. Everyone else can be cast out of the proverbial Rolodex.

Now, how can you tell a good contact in the event that you don't have any results to measure? Not all contacts are the kind of people who promise to deliver something tangible, after all. In these cases good contacts re the kind of people who have a wealth of information to offer you. Most often they come from the same or at least similar backgrounds as you. They're always making real and valuable referrals. They have proven track records. They know (and can demonstrate that knowledge) how to position and guide you to where you want to go. And, most importantly, they can answer your questions and serve as reliable resources on many of the things you need to learn.

My own right network is full of my mentors from academia, colleagues from the field of marketing, and those folks I have deemed my inner circle (my doctoral guide, my accountant/

mentor, my financial planner, a fellow professor and close friend, and my father). Notice the trend in my right network: it's full of people who are experts in my field and people who have services they can offer that help me achieve my goals—people who have the necessary experience, proven track records, and verifiable histories of success. Note also that I rely on my father for advice quite often. It's always good to include a family member in your inner circle because family members know you better than anyone, have exacted the strongest influence on you throughout your life, and can often see the things you see in a different and incredibly valuable light.

As a final point, sometimes it takes a long time to separate the right contacts from the wrong ones. As Dina Marto of Twelve Music Group pointed out, the best way to build the right network is through trial and error, and of course time.

"Many times," she said, "people who promise you things will surprise you with their ulterior motives. But these experiences are exactly what help you grow as a businessperson and develop the right network. When it comes to network building, time is the best tool for effective growth." As Dina smartly suggested, this time can be reduced if you focus as much on yourself and what you're offering as you do on your network. "When I first started in the music industry, my strategy was to make myself as beneficial as possible to the people I met. I wasn't looking to find people who could help me. Instead I was looking for ways I could help the people in my industry."

Sometimes the best way to tell a right contact from a wrong one is to be a right one yourself. It never hurts to flip the game on its head. Don't go out looking to receive something; go out looking to *give something*. In time you will be overwhelmed by the positive results.

Is There a Vetting Process?

Certainly—though it's not an exact science. In the absence of measurable results, the best way to determine the contacts you should pursue, keep, or foster closer relationships with is to examine the ways in which you met these people. My doctoral guide, for instance, became my mentor after years of guiding me through the process of obtaining my doctorate. Over those years I learned he was intelligent, insightful, and knowledgeable about the most effective route between candidate and doctorate, and, from his reputation and many publications in academic journals, I knew he could tell me exactly how to get where I felt I needed to go. Given all that—and the fact that he has become a close friend—it's clear that he is among my most valuable contacts.

In the absence of many years of working closely together, there are always referrals from people you trust. My accountant, for instance, was a referral from my sister. I have learned from experience that my sister is very meticulous in her relationships and is always careful to associate only with the best and brightest. Naturally that meant my accountant could be trusted and brought into my circle. Over the years that followed, he certainly backed up my sister's referral with positive results. He has for a long while been one of my most important business connections.

When in doubt ask yourself if this person has done what you intend to do. Take my fellow professor contact. I knew he would be a good friend to have because he had already created his own network of speaking engagements, written a half dozen books, and built a strong presence online—three of my most visible goals at the time we met. Often the best mentors and the best people for a network are those who have been there and done that. They can tell you what you must do to achieve your goals because they have *already achieved them*. My professor friend gave me invaluable advice on how to build my large Twitter following, how to generate speaking engagements, and even how to write this book.

Perhaps most important is this factor: if this person is to remain in your network, he or she has to be stable—and I mean that in every sense of the word: financially, professionally, socially, etc. Mentors and valuable contacts are only as strong as their bases. They must be proven in their fields. They must be able to demonstrate their expertise. They must be capable of offering the kind of advice or aid you need to make decisions and get things done. And they must be able to do all these things without the distraction that comes from personal turmoil.

So, with all of that in mind, how do you vet your contact pool? By conducting meticulous evaluations of all contact. Ask yourself what these people have done in the past. Ask what they are good at. Ask what kind of clientele they have. Ask how they market themselves. Determine the state and health of their business or career. Figure out how they match up with the competition. Use every measure you can think of to assess their level of success. The goal in building the right network is to keep only those people who show excellence in the majority of these questions. We want a small network full of masters of their crafts.

Identify Your Clients

Incidentally this vetting process works for your client pool as well. Rachel Hollis of

Chic Events suggests that the best way to determine the best members of your client pool is first to identify who your ideal clients are and then identify who your ideal clients are *not*.

"It's important to identify who you're going after because not everybody can be your client," she shared. In other words, if you're a high-end company like Chic Events, you aren't going to meet your summer wedding clients at a bridal expo. Instead you find them by identifying an exceptional photographer and inquiring about referrals for the kind of bride that fits the company profile.

"Part of finding the right network and the kind of people who can connect you with the right client base is just trial and error," she said, echoing Dina Marto. "It's a matter of settling in with the vendors you know you can trust and the business associates you have come to like."

The process can be a long one, unfortunately, but the results are well worth the effort. By now Rachel can pick and choose the clients she works with thanks to her valuable and effective right network. "Life is too short to work with jerks," she said with a laugh. "This job is already stressful enough without having to work with people who only add to the stress." In this way, often

the right clients aren't always the ones with
the most money; they're the ones you enjoy
working with no matter what.

How to Build the Right Network

At its heart the right network works for you and is aligned to
your goals. If you're a woman setting up a business, for instance,
your network might benefit from including other women in
business. Ideally it should include people who have already succeeded in your field or achieved the goals you're setting out to
achieve. And it is always helpful to include members of your
peer group, whether family or close friends, who you can always
trust to be honest and straightforward with you. With that in
mind, consider the following pieces of wisdom I gleaned from
the thirteen successful women (myself included) who contributed to this book:

1. **Be proactive.**
    Building the right network is all about taking action.
    Do not confuse this with the action required by the
    traditional wisdom, however. I'm not calling for you
    to go out and hand out as many business cards as
    you can fit in your pocket. At the same time, don't
    rest on your accomplishments. Many of the women I
    interviewed (and I follow this wisdom as well) try to
    set up meetings with a potential or existing contacts
    at least once per week. Some people like to while
    away their time at their desks, figuring success will

come naturally as long as they work 70 hours per week. But it won't. And your network won't deliver you the results you're looking for if you don't interact with it either.

So once you have vetted your list, reach out to your remaining and potential contacts. Set up face-to-face meetings (face to face point is important; shaking hands is always more effective than sending e-mails) to occur at least once per week. The meetings don't have to be about something specific, either, and they should never be entirely about the help you're seeking. You can just meet to chat and catch up. Often, in these informal meetings, the best and most advantageous connections are struck.

In furthering the effort to make the meetings less formal, consider nontraditional formats and settings. Instead of lunch, meet for breakfast. Meet outside. Meet while walking or working out. Change the setting as often as possible. These varied and shared experiences will further endear you to your contacts and them to you.

2. Reach out.

I can't stress this enough: if your network does not include an expert in your specific field, it is not yet the right network. If you can connect with someone who has lived and achieved your dream already, you will find there are few people in your network more valuable. They can offer you good advice because they've actually seen that advice work before. Further, it's possible they can connect you to more people who might be in positions to help you achieve your goals.

Don't be afraid to reach out to them even if you don't know them at all. There's nothing wrong with reaching out—and there's nothing quite as flattering as being asked advice because you're an expert in your field. As long as this person has extensive experience with what you want to do, and as long as he or she has a proven track record of success, he or she fits your right network, and you should go the extra mile to include him or her.

3. **Social network.**

Certainly there are dangers to relying too heavily on LinkedIn, Twitter, and Facebook, but that doesn't mean they aren't incredibly valuable resources. I owe much of my success to my Twitter following. The trick, though, is the same as it is for standard networking. It's not about the number of friends or followers or contacts you have; it's about the *value* and *relevance* those friends/followers/contacts bring to the table.

To start your social media network, begin by joining up with groups that align with the business you're in. Join as many relevant groups as you can. Then do two things as often as possible. First offer insight via thoughtful posts about things that are relevant to your friends/followers/contacts. One of the chief drivers of my Twitter success has been the inspirational quotes I post each morning. Second, reach out to specific friends/followers/contacts whenever you saw something or have something you can offer them. Give to your network and in time it will give back to you.

4. Benchmark.

As I mentioned in the vetting process, a contact is only as good as his or her measurable results. For this reason it is important to benchmark your contacts in exactly the same way you benchmark your business. Set up a timeframe or when you need to see things done. If the contact does not meet that timeframe, consider moving on. If the promises don't align with the results, it's time to re-strategize.

The people worthy of your right network—especially those who wind up in your inner circle—need to demonstrate results in both the past and present. If they are experts in the field you're pursuing, that is ideal. Most of all they must be people you can trust and rely upon.

With that right network at hand, you are ready to begin putting all of your plans into action. Note that the key word here is *action*. All the planning in the world won't help you—even if you have the right network there for aid—if you don't know how to implement.

Strategy and Implementation Are Symbiotic

Bringer, Battler, Begetter, Builder, Bearer

If I could, I would like to return for a moment to the story of Savannah Britt. Here we have one of the world's youngest publishers, a young woman who, even at the tender age of eighteen, has seen remarkable success in an extremely difficult industry. How in the world has Britt managed to make such a name for herself in the publishing world when so many other publishers are struggling? There has to be an answer for why someone so young could have made so much progress down this otherwise difficult road.

"Plan and execute," she told me in response to my question about her greatest business strategy. She was speaking about a concept I hold near and dear to my heart: all the planning in the world will only get you so far. It's the execution that's important. Or, as Britt pointed out, the execution and the planning need to coexist. You can't have one without the other. If one component is weak, the other will be also. Strategy and implementation are symbiotic.

"I strongly believe in creating a business plan," she shared. "Getting the team together is important. So is having someone backing you in every location—someone spreading your name, your brand, and the good word about your business. Planning is definitely key. But without the execution of your strategy, all that planning goes nowhere."

I asked her if she had any advice specifically on how to plan for an important corporate strategy. "I don't like putting out past projects that are only fifty percent good. I believe in planning well and having a great business plan and great backing behind what you're going to put out. But again, the most important thing is executing. The most important thing is actually *doing* what you say you're going to do."

From my perspective, when I think about the word *strategy*, I take the classic definition. Strategy is the plan of action you develop in order to achieve your vision. It's all about gaining or at least being prepared for a position or an advantage over the competition. It's also about spotting those moments and points in time when you can better yourself. Strategy is the route you take to becoming a winner.

When most people hear the word *strategy*, their minds dart to one of three arenas where the term is commonly used: chess, sports (and in this country, the sport most often referenced is football), and the military. In each arena the strategies look very different but also hold some important similarities. And, in each arena, sound strategy is *essential* to winning. In chess, a game of thought, your strategy must include more foresight and creativity than your opponent's. You must outthink the other player in order to win. In football the same is true, but you must add in a layer of practice and fitness strategy. Good coaches must outmaneuver their counterparts, but good players must outwork the opponent as well. In the military, where lives are on the line, strategy becomes a more important matter. Given the variability of landscapes, political conditions, and enemy cohesiveness and arsenal, strategy has a tendency to be a more fluid and ever-changing matter.

In all cases sound strategy requires diligence and hard work. Whether preparing for a chess match, a football game, or war you must sit down, analyze the opponent, brainstorm outcomes, devise tactics to take advantage of the opponent's weaknesses, and imagine the most logical path to victory. Without this important component, your hopes of winning diminish to almost zero. All good entrepreneurs recognize this fact. It's interesting to note that of the twelve women I interviewed for this book, when asked the simple question of whether they considered themselves strategists, each came back with a quick and resounding "yes." They recognized and celebrated the notion that you don't get anywhere in life without a good strategy.

Take Disney for example. Everyone knows Disney. *Everyone.* As a company it is truly one of the most remarkable and awe-inspiring American success stories. It is in many ways the pinnacle of branding and marketing. And, in true American fashion, it all started as one man's dream. But then even Disney has seen its share of setbacks as a result of improper strategy. Do you remember the fiasco surrounding the initial opening of Euro Disney? If not, let me refresh your memory...

By 1992 The Walt Disney Company had already established wildly profitable parks in two locations in the United States and one in Japan. Given their success—along with the success of the Disney brand and Disney films worldwide—the company assumed it could be repeated anywhere in the world. Using this logic the company speculated it could open a park nearly identical to its Orlando, Florida, location in Paris and become an instant success. This line of thinking was, in a nutshell, completely wrong. Because Disney failed to do its due diligence and perform apt research on the tourism market in Europe and on French sentiment regarding Disneyland, they discovered the hard way that French citizens and Europeans at large were not interested in embracing the exact same theme park as did the Americans and Japanese. Without a strategy for entering that unique market, Euro Disney was a short-term flop. After the park opened its doors, the company began losing money. Euro Disney lost millions of dollars year after year. Where Disney had been prepared to turn an immediate profit, in reality it took them five years just to pull themselves out of the red.

Now, it's one thing if you or I jump into something without sound strategy, but we're talking about an American icon here—a multibillion-dollar company. How could they make that kind of mistake? They did so under the assumption that they were incapable of failing—as if they could simply implement without fully strategizing. When you never take action on your vision, you don't get what you want; the same is true when you go into something blindly.

In earlier chapters we discussed the importance of sound strategy. And I must admit I too am guilty of occasionally making decisions without first devising an appropriate plan. When you dive into something headfirst without considering strengths, weaknesses, opportunities, and threats, it's almost like setting yourself up for failure. At the very least, without a SWOT analysis you're not giving yourself a fair chance to succeed. But that is not the point this chapter attempts to make. Where I would like to go is in the direction of implementation.

To me the word *implementation* means a realization of your plan, idea, strategy, policy, etc. Strategy is your vision for the future; implementation is your 110-percent effort to make that vision a reality. Strategy is dreaming; implementation is doing. Nothing happens without both.

Consider some of the greatest innovations of the technological era in which we live. How about Facebook? If you believe the stories that have arisen about the litigation in the background of the company, or if you just enjoyed the recounting of the events in the movie about it, you can see pretty clearly that an idea is nothing without the ability to implement it. If you're unfamiliar, the rumor is that Facebook was actually the idea of another couple of gentlemen who went to Harvard with Mark Zuckerberg, founder of Facebook. If that's true, then these two gentlemen were the source of one of the most brilliant business ideas and strategies of the current century. The only trouble is they apparently didn't have the resources at the time to turn their dream into a reality. Enter Zuckerberg, who clearly did not suffer from the same shortfall. He supposedly took this brilliant idea and, through his own ingenuity, foresight, and coding genius, implemented it into the multibillion-dollar reality it has become.

Or, if you prefer an example more rooted in verifiable fact, consider Google. It wasn't the first search engine. Driving profit by becoming the vehicle for finding things on the Internet was not an original idea. Yahoo! was already well entrenched when Google first hit the scene, and Yahoo! wasn't even the first search engine online.

What made Google the global technology giant it has become was not the idea side of the strategy-implementation synergy; it was the implementation. Google figured out how to do it better, more efficiently, and in a more user-friendly way than Yahoo! Then, when Google had taken root in the market, they proved again and again that nobody on the planet implements a brilliant idea better or faster. Now they're not just providers of the world's most popular search engine; they're cataloguing the sum of human knowledge, creating the most detailed maps in history, speculating in space travel, and even building cars that drive themselves. What allows them to do these things where so many other innovative companies have failed is that they know how to *implement*.

How to Unify Your Strategy and Implementation Processes

So how can you avoid a Euro Disney disaster? How can you become more like the Googles of the world, for whom implementation and strategy share equal importance and focus? There are many steps to consider, and they all depend on what kind of strategy you hope to implement, but the following should have a place at the table no matter who you are or what you intend to do.

- **Do not procrastinate.**
  It doesn't matter what brand of business model you're using, and it doesn't matter what phase of the game you find yourself in; procrastination can be the biggest killer of any strategy. If you haven't yet taken the time to create a business plan, what are you waiting for? If you've got your plan in place but you haven't set the ball in motion on finding funding, what are you waiting for? If you've got the funding and the

assets you need to put your strategy in motion, what are you waiting for?

Taking it slowly and wanting to make sure you've considered every variable is one thing. Using that as an excuse for inaction is entirely another. Many times we'll say, "Yeah, I want this, and I have these wonderful ideas, and this is how I'm going to make them happen," but then we never make them happen. As I've said in previous chapters, this is often the result of fear. But, in its simplest form, it can also be the result of an addiction to procrastination. It's so very easy to put off until tomorrow what can be done today, but no great entrepreneur or executive ever made a habit out of that.

So stop thinking so much because you're too worried about what the competition is doing. Stop talking about how great your idea is and start doing what needs to happen today to get things up and running. Don't dwell on the why-you-can't. Concentrate on the why-you-can.

- **Prepare a budget.**
  For entrepreneurs everything tends to start and end with money. No strategy is complete without properly accounting for an accurate financial projection. No implementation works if it suffers from a substantial financial shortfall. Let's say you need $30,000 to start your business. If you don't have it, you need to strategize how you're going to get it. Now, let's say you *have* $30,000 to start your business. If you don't put that money to work wisely, your strategy

isn't going to carry you through to the end of the implementation phase.

Write a thorough business plan. Pitch it to the people you need for financial or conceptual help. Go after angel investors. If you're fortunate enough to have family and friends who are wealthy or talented enough to help, ask for their help. Don't fear money. It is surely the ultimate means to making your dream a reality, but it also has a tendency to begin feeling like an obstacle. With a sound business plan in place, you can head into your implementation with the knowledge that the money will be there when you need it (and, at the very least, you'll have contingency plans in place in the event the money begins to grow tight).

The People We Love, the People We Trust

Juliette Brindak had a dream from a very young age. That dream was to provide a haven for young girls to be themselves. In this way Miss O & Friends was born. But, as Brindak learned early on, that idea would not become a reality without careful implementation—and that began with asking for startup funding. Now Brindak is a very smart and capable businesswoman, but she admitted to me that she would not have gotten to where she is today without the help of her parents. Her mother and father believed so much in their young daughter's idea they helped her prepare a pitch presentation, then reached out to everyone in their networks who were in positions to help, and began setting up meetings for Brindak to pitch her idea.

They came up against resistance at first. "We would pitch to different people—investment groups and VCs mostly," she explained. "The problem we found was that they were all men. Unless they had daughters or nieces, they didn't get what we were doing. They just thought that this was some dumb company for girls, and since it wasn't about technology or medicine, they didn't care about it."

But again Brindak and her parents believed in the company so much they did not stop trying. That was when a new sense of strategy began. "When we found the people who believed in what we were doing for young girls, we latched on to them," she explained, laughing. "We offered equity, board positions, whatever we had to do to get them onboard. We knew that in the absence of being able to do this all on our own, we would need people of like mindset or at least people operating under the same umbrella."

So take a lesson from Juliette. When it comes time to implement a strategy, never be afraid to rely on the people you love, and never hesitate to bring into the fold the people you trust.

———

- **Tell yourself, "I really don't have a choice."**
  This piece of advice is perhaps the one thing that keeps me going whenever I'm faced with a new business concept or even just the prospect of change. It's the mantra I use to help me overcome the fear associated with taking the leap. If you keep your mindset focused on the "what ifs" and the doubts, you'll never get anywhere. But if you can successfully convince yourself that you have no choice but to take the leap, you will be implementing effectively in no time.

  In life we can face many obstacles, but more often than not the only thing holding us back is ourselves. So, instead of talking about why you can't do it, start talking about all the reasons you *should* or *can* do it. Strategy is the act of coming up with something new and different. Implementing is a matter of taking this huge step into the unknown. So the most effective way to marry your strategy and your implementation is to talk yourself into the strategy's validity and the implementation's inevitable success.

Just Take the Job Already

If you're thinking about switching careers, what's stopping you? The economy? This can be overcome. Waiting for that bonus? How much money is your happiness worth? A better opportunity to open up? What if it doesn't? How long are you willing to hold out?

The bottom line is: if you're thinking about switching careers because you are unhappy or even because you don't see yourself doing this same line of work five to seven years from now, there's no reason to wait around. Just take that first step. Start sending out your résumé. Go on interviews. Sit in on teleconferences with prospective employers. Research the things you will need to know to begin a career in a new field. If the move will require you to travel to a different region of the country or world, go to visit your potential new jobsite. Eliminate everything that could be standing in the way of landing that new job. Stop masking your fears with a need to spend more time strategizing. Start implementing.

- **Have a contingency plan.**

  Nine times out of ten, a strategy fails because it failed to take into account all possible negative outcomes. The surest way to submit to this common failure is to go into your implementation phase without at least one fallback plan. No amount of planning can predict every possible outcome, so why pretend any of us is capable of leaping into a situation with perfect foresight? We've all heard the importance of going in with a plan A, a plan B, and a plan C, yet many of us tend to approach even the most major situations in our lives with only a plan A.

  If you're looking for funding for your startup, you need to be saying things like, "If the angel investors don't work out, I'll go to the small business bureau. If not the SBB, then I will approach my family and friends. If my family and friends can't help, I'll get a second job." Yet many of us give up on our ideas because we wind up thinking, *Ugh, the angel investors just couldn't see the big picture. I guess I'll have to go back to a nine-to-five.*

  In all honesty I have seen several setbacks in my own career path. And one of the most common themes from my interviews for this book was that setbacks are abundantly common. It's not a matter of whether you will make mistakes or encounter unforeseen outcomes; it's a matter of how you deal with them. If you beat yourself up over the failure of plan A, you'll never get anywhere. If you immediately switch to implementing plan B, progress will continue. So be proactive as you strategize, and be reactive as you implement. Do this and your strategy and implementation structure will move forward with greater harmony.

The business world is full of stories about genius ideas that didn't become realities because the innovators didn't properly strategize. For every failure-in-strategy story, there is an equal number of failure-in-implementation stories. The common theme in all of them is that there just wasn't enough attention paid to one or the other. If you look across the landscape of the hundreds of thousands of successful businesses in this country, you will find one common theme: strategy and implementation were symbiotic.

Another common theme is this: the successful businesses, and the successful nine-to-fivers for that matter, achieve their success because they do it better than the competition. In some cases that means better strategy or better implementation. In some cases that means better marketing or a higher-quality product or service. In still others the success is the result of the business leader's genius and his or her ability to rewrite the game so completely as to render the competition irrelevant. Read on to learn how to do something much more than just beat the competition; learn how to run your company or your career in such a way that what the competition does or doesn't do simply does not matter.

Create Your Own Blue Ocean

Brutal, Bright, Boastful, Blue, Brassy

We still have a couple of chapters to go before we get into the subject of inspiration and what it means to the successful woman, but let me tell you about a book I once read that changed my life. Given the book's international best-seller status, I'm guessing I'm not the only person who had such an experience upon reading it.

First a little background: Before I read the book that changed my life back in 2005, I was under the mistaken impression that in order to succeed I had to *beat* the competition. I had to figure out what the competition was doing, then determine how to do it better. In that thought I was not alone as well. I knew back then that if I worked hard, worked smart, and demonstrated to the consumer that I was the best choice in a sea of choices for marketing experts, I would come out on top eventually.

Oh, how I was wrong. W. Chan Kim and Renée Mauborgne's brilliant *Blue Ocean Strategy* (Harvard Business School Publishing Corporation, 2005) opened my eyes to a new and entirely different outlook on competition and product/service

positioning. In short they taught me—and millions of others—
that "[t]he only way to beat the competition is to stop *trying*
to beat the competition." I could not have been more intrigued
when I first learned of this concept. All my life I had been
spending my time and energy on determining how to better my
counterparts. This book taught me that the only competition
that matters is *me.*

Tai Beauchamp agrees. "I don't believe in outside competition," she told me. "I'm my own competition. The only person
I'm up against is me." That's the Blue Ocean Strategy in a nutshell, and the sooner you can learn to embrace the concept that
the only person you need to worry about competing with is
yourself, the sooner you will find yourself rising above every
other business or person who does something similar to what
you do.

But let's take a step back for a moment. Let's define what it
means to operate in a blue ocean. As Kim and Mauborgne suggest, there are two kinds of oceans in the business world. There
are red oceans and there are blue oceans. In a red ocean "the
industry boundaries are defined and accepted, and the competitive rules of the game are known." This is your standard realm
of competition. Here you have every competitor doing roughly
the same thing in roughly the same way. Every competitor takes
a relatively conventional approach to doing business and tries
to leverage that conventional approach in such a way as to beat
the competition. That all seems nice and standard and predictable. Building a defensible strategy in such an ocean can be an
incredibly clear-cut matter for all those who are willing to work
hard and do their research. But a red ocean has its dangers. In
these oceans, sometimes the strongest and smartest survive, but
sometimes it's just a matter of being lucky. There are so many

competitors—and the competition is so deadly fierce—that the best and the brightest don't always succeed. Sometimes the best and brightest get shredded by all the sharks.

For this reason the authors advocate a strategy that concentrates not on how to win in the predictable but fierce red oceans. Rather they promote the concept of creating your own blue ocean—a place where *you* are the only real competitor because your products or services are so unique that competition becomes irrelevant. Or, as Kim and Mauborgne put it, "[i]n blue oceans, competition is irrelevant because the rules of the game are waiting to be set."

Try to imagine that. Try to imagine a business environment where you don't have to worry even for a moment about what the competition is doing. Try to imagine spending all of your time and energy not on trying to do it better than the competition but rather on trying to better yourself. If my life and work experiences are any indication, this utopia is realistic and entirely achievable. "The creators of blue oceans, surprisingly, didn't use the competition as their benchmark," Kim and Mauborgne write. "...Instead of focusing on beating the competition, they focus on making the competition irrelevant by creating a *leap in value* for buyers and your company, thereby opening up new and uncontested market space."

You know what's interesting about this revolutionary Blue Ocean Strategy? It seemed to come naturally to just about every successful woman I interviewed for this book. It appears that one of the differences between entrepreneurs who succeed and entrepreneurs who flail around for answers is that the former spend almost none of their time on matters of external competition. Take Erica Diamond for example. "In my business, it doesn't matter what the competition does because there's really only one you in this world." In other words, instead of concentrating on what differentiates herself from the competition, she has instead decided to rely on one simple and undeniable fact: no one (no one!) can do what Erica Diamond does in exactly the same way Erica Diamond does it.

And she is not alone. "I don't believe in competition," Rachel Hollis told me. "I have a specific style. I'm a specific person. If you're hiring me to do something, I'm going to do it in a way that only I can. Whatever the competition is doing, I'm not paying attention to it. To me, if you identify yourself and your style—and your brand is different and unique and special enough—then there *is* no competition because nobody is going to do it like you do."

What about those who prefer to remain in a more predictable environment? What about those who would rather maintain the status quo, work within the rules, and shape strategies that may or may not lead to success in a red ocean? On its surface one can make a compelling case for sticking with the norm. However, when we dig deeper into the nature of competition, it becomes clear that such a strategy can be incredibly damaging in ways not often seen.

Let's think about how it affects the entrepreneur. Competition can do a couple of things to a business. It can provide you with a false sense of what the industry is. Think about it: if we're trying to determine market needs, health, and trends by studying everything the competition is doing, how can we possibly expect to get an accurate picture of anything? What we're studying isn't industry truth; it's the competition's propaganda. Nobody in their right mind would paint themselves in a negative light on their website or in their marketing materials.

So, in conducting much of your research into the health and

strategies of your competitors, you might be getting a picture that's healthier than reality. What this means is that when you're swimming in a red ocean, it's difficult to get an accurate gauge on what the market is really about.

Another danger comes from the established industry rules. Red oceans require certain rules and standards that your business might not actually need to compete with and/or consider. These rules might be accepted by most of the established sharks, but they might actually be holding you back as you try to gain entry into the market. Think about it: if you own an established business in a given industry—let's say you make cookies—and you've been doing this business for a decade, what's your incentive to create rules that level the playing field? As a person with power and influence in that given industry—and as a person who really enjoys making money from all your established customers—wouldn't you do what you can to establish rules that make it *more difficult* for startup bakeries to take hold in your market? I know I would. Protecting the things that provide for you is an animal instinct. It's a call to self-preservation. It makes perfect sense to want to stack the deck in your favor.

So there's your red ocean, entrepreneurs. You have an environment that creates confusion about market trends and competitor health, and you have rules that were *set by the competition*, rules that will make it more difficult for you to succeed. Sure, if you study the market and the competition long enough, you might be able to find some leverage—or a *niche*, as traditional business strategies call it—but who would want to do that? Not me. Not the twelve women I interviewed for this book. Not when there's that nice, lush blue ocean awaiting us on the other side.

Maybe you're not an entrepreneur. Maybe you're a

nine-to-fiver who wants to move up the ladder at work. You might be thinking the Blue Ocean Strategy doesn't apply to you. You are, after all, surrounded by an environment with pre-established rules and a large group of coworkers all competing for the same promotion. That's one way to think about it. Another way to think about it is like this: it doesn't matter what my coworkers do because none of them can do anything in exactly the same why I do it. In other words your Blue Ocean Strategy can be to concentrate not on how your coworker nailed his or her last presentation but rather on how to make *your* next presentation incredibly memorable.

Many times in an office setting, those with upward aspirations will try to emulate the person they think is the frontrunner in the organization. Sometimes that means doing things exactly like the coworker competing for the same promotion you would like. Sometimes that means pretending to be just like the person who holds the job you would like to one day fill. It's not that this strategy never works; it's just so inauthentic. More often than not, the decision makers at the firm will recognize when you're not being true to yourself. Sometimes that lack of authenticity shows up in your work product without your even realizing it.

The bottom line is that whether we're starting a business or trying to get that promotion at work, we can never truly know what is the absolute and guaranteed inside track. There are always ethical issues that can arise when we try to emulate the competition. And there are always dangers when we provoke the competition. The better strategy is to remove yourself from these concerns. The better strategy is to form and maintain your own unique standards, and determine what you will and won't do.

Keeping Up with the Joneses

If the blue ocean is so much more attractive than the red ocean, why do so many people have a tendency to stick with that focus on external competition? In short, it's human nature. Nearly everyone feels that need to see how they measure up to other people. That ego needs to be fed, after all. If we hope to see how we're doing on a given task or personal trait, the best and simplest way to find the answer is to examine how other people are doing it. It's the old "keeping up with the Joneses" routine. The neighbor hires landscapers to create a terraced yard, so we have to hire landscapers to construct an elaborate garden. The neighbor buys a high-end riding lawnmower, so we have to do the same. The neighbor gets a new SUV, so we have to get a new sports car. Our need to feel like the best of the best can become more destructive than constructive.

Many people fall into this trap. It's just so easy to focus too much of your time on worrying about others and too little on what you're doing yourself. More destructive still is the fact that we always tend to "compare our very worst to someone else's very best," as Erica Diamond said. "It becomes a spirit crusher and a nightmare for you."

Her solution? Stop thinking about bettering the competition and start thinking about bettering yourself. The only time Erica ever examines the competition is to determine little ways to tweak what she is already doing. She never uses it to influence her direction. "There's only one person like you," she reminds. "Only one person who can give this specific output. That's differentiation built in right there."

So how did Erica overcome her own inherent tendency to keep up with the Joneses? "Everyone was opening up a business like mine in their basement. They were all penny pinching for the best price. But I realized my business wasn't going to grow if I kept trying to get better and doing the same things the competition did. My business would only grow because of me. WomenOnTheFence.com has grown not because of some magical solution but because of Erica Diamond."

For Erica it doesn't matter what the Joneses do. It doesn't even matter how many Joneses there are. You can find yourself surrounded by people who do exactly what you hope to do in your business or at your workplace. With the Blue Ocean Strategy in mind, "you can start a company in a sea of competition, but it is you that will make you stand out."

How to Create Your Own Blue Ocean

Now that you understand the value of creating your own blue ocean, we can shift our attention toward figuring out a strategy that will work for you. Creating my own blue ocean was a matter of focusing not on what the competition was doing but on all the ways I was different from the competition. I did everything I could to make myself nothing like the status quo. And I mean this very literally. When I did the research, I gathered the stats and then spent all my time thinking about how I could make myself the exact opposite of the trend. It was like when I graduated with my doctorate and all my colleagues were trying to become professors at traditional universities. Instead of swimming in that red ocean—instead of competing against the very same people I called friends—I was going to swim away into my own blue ocean. I was going to do what it took to use my marketing and innovative skills in every way possible. For me that meant becoming a marketing professor in an online classroom in conjunction with serving my marketing clients at my marketing firm.

In the end I differentiated myself in such a way that the Dr. Kay brand emerged naturally. I built that brand based not on what I thought the market wanted. Rather I built it based on my unique personality, strengths, passion, and education. Plenty of people do what I do, but none of them do it in exactly the same way I do. My own blue ocean came to be because I was not afraid to be my authentic self.

When I realized this, the many benefits of swimming in my own blue ocean came to me all at once. I knew I could operate with authenticity in any meeting. I knew I would create real value for my clients. I was free enough to be able to demonstrate true innovation. New doors began to open for me in the marketplace. I was able to reach customers I never could have reached before. The boundaries that once had confined me completely disappeared. And, most importantly, competition became irrelevant.

I have enjoyed these advantages for seven years. Now I would like to pass them on to you by sharing some steps to consider when creating your own blue ocean.

1. **Redirect your focus.**

   Let's allow Kim and Mauborgne to start us off: "To fundamentally shift the strategy canvas of an industry, you must begin by reorienting your strategic focus *from* competitors to alternatives, and from customers to non-customers of an industry." In other words stop trying to be like your competition and start demonstrating how you're the valuable alternative. Stop trying to woo the customers away from the competition and start looking for your own brand of customer. Remember, the goal here is not to figure out how to fit into an established market. It's about creating an environment in which you are the only competitor—an environment in which you are the go-to person for your product or service.

That's not to say you should delude yourself into thinking you're the only one around. It means you should start thinking about yourself as the best and brightest. Do this and the customer base will naturally follow. "As you shift your strategic focus from current competition to alternatives and non-consumers, you gain insight into how to redefine the problem the industry focuses on and thereby reconstruct buyer value elements that reside across industry boundaries." In other words if you turn your focus inward, you'll be much more likely to become the next innovator who changes the market—and who wouldn't want to be that next innovator?

For an entrepreneur, redirecting the focus means ignoring a competitor's predefined rules and values and starting to broaden your understanding of what your value is. Don't worry about what other people bring to the table for the customer; worry about what *you* bring to the table. Then, when you have clearly defined your strengths and all those things that make you who you are, you can begin to look at ways to accentuate that for your prospective customers. This goes back to building your brand. It shouldn't center around why you're better than the rest; it should highlight what makes you who you are. Make it clear to your customers that you have a favorable personality and have authentic strengths that might work for them, and they will select you in a more organic way.

If you're a nine-to-fiver, the trick is to do things to make yourself more authentic. If you're competing with someone else, you only have to be better than that person. If you're competing with yourself, you're trying to improve yourself holistically. The latter leads to more positive momentum and longer-term personal gain.

2. Build a culture of improvement.
The best way to break free from the bonds of our natural competitive nature is to concentrate all our energy on improving ourselves. Like the entrepreneur building a new business, we must never be satisfied with past achievements. No matter what we have done and no matter how much we have gained, we have to keep looking for ways to get better. We can't just rest on our accomplishments. We have to get up, keep moving, and keep improving.

If you can learn to embrace this mindset, then not only will you find yourself swimming in your own blue ocean; you will find it's nearly impossible for any new competition to join you. You'll be unique and effective, and getting better at what you do every single day.

3. Be okay with no.
We've already discussed the importance of finding ways to overcome those many no's in life, but the concept bears repeating here. If you're truly going to ignore what the competition is doing, you have to accept the fact that sometimes the competition will just be a better fit for certain people. You have to understand that no's are natural.

"I'm the first person to say I'm not for everybody," Rachel Hollis shared with me. "You might want someone who wears a suit and is more conservative than I am. And that's fine. I would rather work with the people who value my brand." This is perhaps the most difficult psychological leap for most people to make when they attempt to create their own blue oceans. Part of being unique is understanding that not everyone will value or even agree with what you're doing. Let those people go. It wasn't a good fit anyway. As long as you're swimming in your own blue ocean, the customers that make sense for you will come.

4. Don't compete and defeat.

The second most difficult psychological leap has to be tearing yourself away from that natural tendency to want to be better than the competition. We're natural competitors. Competition is how every species on the planet survives. But in business it can be incredibly destructive. How do we turn competition into something more constructive?

"My strategy is to collaborate and talk rather than compete and defeat," Kanini Mutooni explained. "Collaboration has much more potential for you to gain because you can learn something you don't know. The bonus is that the other person can gain from the collaboration as well. Collaboration is much more profitable and productive than fighting and working at loggerheads."

Kanini makes an excellent point. The thing about

business is that customers are going to go with their preferences no matter what we do. If we can figure out ways to bridge gaps with the competition—and even go so far as to do the unthinkable and *work with* the competition—we might find ourselves in better positions to reach more customers than we ever could before. The same is true at a nine-to-five job. Instead of trying to better your competitor for that promotion, working with him or her might improve your chances of getting noticed by the folks who do the hiring.

5. **Focus on the bigger picture.**
    If we're truly swimming in our own blue oceans, the rigors of that old red ocean no longer apply. So instead of trying to figure out how we can adapt the old rules to our new and unique strategies, we must focus on the bigger picture. In both our strategies and our value propositions, we must attempt to go beyond what is expected in the market. We must ignore all boundaries and examine our new environment as if it is limitless.

    The cookie-cutter approach doesn't work for everything. What worked in the old environment might not necessarily work in the new. Your goal in focusing on the bigger picture should be to figure out how your authentic strengths and your authentic values might apply to a market that is far larger and much less refined than the one you left. Don't be afraid to do things differently. Don't be afraid to be yourself. And don't be afraid to accept clients from backgrounds you never could have anticipated.

6. Declare your independence.

The truly beautiful thing that lies at the center of this strategy is independence. You're not just positioning yourself advantageously in the marketplace; you're freeing yourself from the shackles of competition and rules. You are completely and utterly independent. Cherish that fact.

One of the greatest things about the Dr. Kay brand and swimming in my own blue ocean is that I'm not a full-time agent for anyone. Everything I've done and will continue to do, whether it's creating my résumé, contracting out to other companies, or building my consulting firm, will be utterly independent. To keep myself in my own blue ocean, I will never tie myself down to any one opportunity or any one customer. I will do things my way, and my way will continue to lead to success.

So now that you're independent, use it to your advantage. Because you don't have the same rules as everyone else, don't be afraid to shake it up. Innovate wherever possible. Project your value onto the world. And never stop learning, growing, adapting, and evolving. Once you have found success, there are going to be people or businesses that try to emulate what you do. Part of remaining in that blue ocean is never resting or becoming satisfied with that you do.

You swim along in your own blue ocean. The

unfettered nature of that fact is an incredible competitive advantage. Use that to keep bettering yourself, and it will always remain.

The bottom line when creating your own blue ocean is that in order to succeed—in order to attract customers, or in order to land that big promotion—you must always concentrate on delivering value. Always. The trick here is that while your competition continues to spend all of his or her time and effort trying to figure out how to be better than you, you'll be trying to figure out how to maximize the value you bring to the table. He or she will be worried about your performance; you'll be worried only about how to better yourself. In the end it will be this factor above all others—your concentration on yourself and the value you have to offer—that will lead to success.

Follow the Path to Self-Actualization

Beginner, Blunt, Boisterous, Broad, Beneficiary

Let's turn the search inward for a moment. Over the course of ten rules, I have presented wisdom from a mixed bag of external and internal self-improvement strategies. Many of these strategies were designed to help an aspiring business owner to find success in the entrepreneurial field. Other strategies will benefit nine-to-fivers. Still others are sure to help those among us trying to find jobs in these difficult times. Here I would like to examine a philosophy so rooted in the psychology of success that it is bound to help anyone no matter who they are, where they are from, or what they intend to do with their lives.

In 1943, in a scholarly paper entitled "A Theory of Human Motivation," Abraham Maslow first proposed a concept commonly referred to as the *hierarchy of needs*. The hierarchy is basically a pyramid model that categorizes the stages of growth for all human beings. The most rudimentary stages lie near the bottom (and therefore wider) sections of the pyramid while the most advanced stage (self-actualization, hence the title of this chapter) lies at the top. In general Maslow found that the most successful, influential, and inspiring among us have achieved that top level of the pyramid. They have self-actualized, and in that have met with success in almost every aspect of their lives.

Now, to arrive at this model Maslow examined the lives of people like Eleanor Roosevelt, Frederick Douglass, and Albert Einstein, but that does not mean the hierarchy applies only to the world's most groundbreaking people. No, it is both Maslow's belief and mine that we all follow our own paths along the spectrum of achievement represented in the pyramid. It matters only how completely we dedicate ourselves to achieving the personal and psychological greatness that lies at the top.

Before I outline my own thoughts on how one might best make the climb to the top of the pyramid, let's first take a quick look at the stages as described by Maslow. From lowest to highest on the pyramid, the stages include: physiological, safety, love/belonging, esteem, and self-actualization. I won't get into tremendous detail about each level, but let us at least get an idea of the kinds of things we achieve when we graduate between each tier.

At the physiological level, we all concentrate on and achieve the things that literally keep us alive. Here we have our baser instincts and drives for food, water, sex, and sleep. Natural human functions like breathing and digesting exist on this level as well. Obviously every able-bodied human being achieves these drives naturally. They occupy a greater percentage of the mind and energy for some people than for others, but at the very least we can all agree they are needed just to survive and to realize success at the simplest human level.

The next tier of the pyramid is safety. At this level we have found comfort and success in all of the drives and instincts that keep us alive. Having achieved these needs, we may now turn to securing them. When it comes to safety, we're talking about security in every sense, from the obvious safety of body (prevention from hurting oneself), to the financial safety that comes from secure employment, to the familial safety that comes from stable resources, health, property, and even morality. Not until one achieves a feeling of total safety in each of these important categories can he or she advance to the next stage in the pyramid.

That stage is love/belonging. Now here is perhaps the second most important of the five stages of Maslow's hierarchy, because this is often the category where most people feel content to remain. By this point you have secured all of your primal and many of your earthly needs, and have even gone on to find security in your family, friendships, and sexual intimacy. It's so easy to feel comfortable in this stage because you no longer feel threatened by forces beyond your own power. You have settled down, placed your roots, and started your family, and can find some measure of happiness in the experiences you share with the people around you. This is an exceedingly comfortable stage at which to operate. That comfort causes many, many people to remain right where they are.

But this isn't a book for people who only want comfort. This is a book for people who can see themselves taking the leap to the next and highest two levels of Maslow's hierarchy of needs. If you are such a person—and if you've made it this far in the book, it's safe to assume you are indeed—then you are already most likely churning your way through the esteem tier of the hierarchy.

Of all the women I interviewed for this book, nearly all of them professed the belief that this is right where they currently resided. This is a remarkable revelation in that it demonstrates just how self-aware many successful entrepreneurs tend to be.

These twelve women recognize their own success, but they are also conscious enough about their achievements to realize there is still much work to be done. Like you—and like millions of other people—these twelve women continue to work on achieving comfort with their self-esteem, achievement, confidence, respect of others, and respect *from* others. This can be a difficult stage to master, but it is my firm belief that step one in doing so is to admit you still have a great deal of work to do before you achieve self-actualization. This is why so many of the women interviewed for this book—and so many successful entrepreneurs as a whole—are destined to achieve that illusive top tier of the pyramid.

So now we have reached that top tier of Maslow's hierarchy of needs: self-actualization. Here we achieve a number of incredibly important traits that turn a struggling entrepreneur to a successful one—traits that launch businesses and turn them into household names. In the self-actualization phase—a phase to which we should all aspire—we achieve expert control of our creativity, spontaneity, and problem-solving skills. We have assumed a comfortable and sensible morality. And we operate with the ability to separate fact from fiction while eliminating prejudice. It is, in its own way, the clearest definition of what it means to be enlightened as a person and as an entrepreneur. Everything begins to make perfect sense, and everything begins to come more easily.

Most people never reach the point of self-actualization—at least not fully. Most hover somewhere between love/belonging and esteem. Others languish at the top levels of esteem without ever completely actualizing. It is indeed a select few who achieve the level to which this chapter motivates. It is my great hope that with the advice from my contributors and with the steps outlined in this chapter, you will begin your path toward that ultimate goal.

For me that goal is the culmination of everything we strive for in life. And yet, while it is a culmination, we must not think of it as the endpoint. Rather we must think of it as a peak or, more appropriately, a plateau—that moment at which we reach our highest point and continue along our journey toward becoming the best men and women we can be. Life is, after all, a continuous process, a constant evolution (at least ideally). We must continually enhance ourselves. We must never become one-dimensional in our achievements. We must always work to progress, enhance, and grow.

The thirteen women who contributed to this book (myself included) understand that concept. They know that when you conquer one thing, you must move on to the next. Take Kyle Smitley, for example. With Barley & Birch, she has created a wildly successful organic clothing line for children, but she did not let that become the culmination of her entrepreneurial life. As she explained to me, she's just not built that way. "If I'd said five years ago that when I'm thirty, I want to have a multimillion-dollar company, and I had settled for that, it would have been silly because now I want four multimillion-dollar companies."

To achieve self-actualization, when we conquer one thing, we must move on to the next. We must continually strive to improve ourselves. But all the while, we must also do everything we can to maintain the principles and practices that have made us a success in the first place. Rather than abandon what has worked for us in order to embrace new things, we must instead do our best to add on to what has already worked. We don't change as entrepreneurs and inspired women; we *evolve*.

We must also avoid falling into the trap of routine. When we get used to operating at the basic levels, our wheels tend to spin, and we don't make any real progress. It might seem like a given to say that in order to find success we must do more than simply dwell in the physiological and safety levels of the hierarchy. But then try to recall the darkest time of your life. I know I've been in positions where I was so upset and overwhelmed by life the routine of just safely breathing, eating, and sleeping seemed as comforting as a warm blanket. And when we fail at any given thing, it can be incredibly easy to retreat into the embrace of our families and relish their comforting words. Unfortunately no one ever got anywhere by being comfortable and safe. Every successful entrepreneur or nine-to-fiver got to where they are because they were willing to take a chance at some point or another. For many, those chances were frequent and dramatic.

Love Is Only the Start

Love is a wonderful thing to have, but self-actualization and ultimate personal achievement require quite a bit more than love. In fact, according to the hierarchy, love only gets you halfway there. It isn't what it takes to achieve life's greatest accomplishments. It merely helps you to find contentment. For many people contentment is enough.

But why? Why is it so many people are content to live in the love/belonging tier? Well, it's simple: some people aren't entirely motivated to succeed or to evolve as people. Some seek only external pleasures. Some seek only safety. Some are not internally motivated. Some focus only on one particular thing. Some find themselves content to usher their own unfulfilled aspirations on to their children. Some just take comfort in their families, their jobs, and the routines of their lives. Whatever the case, in order to reach the self-actualization tier, you must strive for more than love and belonging.

"So what?" you might ask. "If a person is content with only love/belonging, what's the need to move on?" It's a compelling question, but it misses the mark slightly. Certainly there are plenty of people who can find happiness in this tier. The vast majority of people do, in fact. But you're not reading this book to be average. You're reading this book because you want to achieve greatness. If you're looking for complete fulfillment that addresses *all* your needs beyond the physical and emotional, needs that extend into the psychological and matters of self, then progress is the name of the game.

Staying in the love/belonging tier is the same as saying you're content to do this same thing in exactly this same way for the rest of your life. You might have grand ideas or even dreams, but you'll never pursue them in a satisfying way. The worst part for the dreamer who remains in the love/belonging tier is all those "what ifs." This person spends his or her whole life thinking things like *What if I'd started that business? What if I'd gotten that degree? What if I'd taken that promotion?* and *What if I'd just taken that leap of faith?* Sure, there will always be comfort in love and belonging, but in it you will never reach your fullest potential, and you will never find the answer to "what if?"

So yes, enjoy your family and friends. Yes, relish the love you have. Yes, give as much love as possible. But also understand there are two levels beyond this stage. The life of the dreamer needs to progress.

To fully conquer the esteem tier, we must reach a level of achievement and mastery that leads to our respecting ourselves and receiving respect from others. With the ten rules that have preceded this one, you have begun to beat your path toward that achievement, mastery, and respect. You have laid out your Blueprint for finding career fulfillment, the love of a family, and respect from your community. As you continue along this path, you will be recognized for your achievements.

At this point—provided that you have followed the steps outlined below—you might be ready to make the leap into self-actualization. Here, you will have become 110-percent comfortable with yourself. You will have accepted your short-comings and adapted to favor all of your strengths. You will be the ultimate realist: a person who knows the difference between fact and carefully crafted fiction. You will be fulfilled not just in your career and family, but in your morality, creativity, and spontaneity as well. You will be the ultimate you, and as a result you will shine in ways you never thought possible.

Imagine a life full of confidence and yet also full of dreams and aspirations. Imagine boundless creativity and ability to innovate. Imagine daily holistic improvement of self. Imagine being able always to see and implement the strategies most likely to work. Imagine better critical thinking, more dynamic decision making, and a more open mind. Imagine all the greatest qualities of you emerging to take control of your life. It all might sound like some feel-good self-help seminar, but it is actually possible. More than that the drive is *innate*. The potential to self-actualize is something that lies within us all. We must only make ourselves willing to progress and then take the steps necessary to unlock that self-actualization.

1. **Stop measuring yourself against others.**
   Most of us have the tendency to measure our self-worth by comparing our accomplishments and abilities to those of the people around us. It's only natural. If we want to see how we're doing, the easiest way is to see how we measure up to our counterparts. It's the surest way to demonstrate how far along we are on the path to achieving success. If we're farther than others, we deem ourselves achievers. If we're not, we tend to stress and work on ways to improve.

   The problem is that self-actualization doesn't have anything to do with the people around us. Notice the *self* part of the term. The only thing that matters is *our* progress, not the progress of others. If we hope to self-actualize, or at least to get on the path to self-actualization, we must stop gauging ourselves against other people's accomplishments. Whether it's education or material things or even beauty standards, we must throw all of that out the window. We must not work from a standpoint of how we compare; rather we must work from a standpoint of where we are personally and independently of everyone else.

To achieve this step, you must be able to look in the mirror and say, "This is my portrait. This is who I am. This is my canvas." With that in mind, do everything in your power not to let the opinions of others color that canvas. Only you can paint the picture of who you want to be. No one else is in control of your destiny. What your competition has done or what your naysayers have said does not matter. Only you matter.

2. Learn to accept yourself holistically.
It's so easy to become dissatisfied with who we are and what we have accomplished. Often times, when we look in the mirror, it actually serves to increase the negativity with which we think about ourselves. We cannot fall into that trap. In order to self-actualize, you must accept your *whole* self. Your strengths and weaknesses, you must embrace them all. We cannot downplay our weaknesses or exaggerate our strengths if we hope to get anywhere in life. If progress is to be made, we must operate first from truth.

We all know people who constantly say things

like, "I wish I could do this" and, "I wish I could do that," but then don't do anything about it. Maybe we are like those people. But we should have learned from a very young age that wishing gets you nowhere. The only way to improve—and certainly the only way to begin to self-actualize—is to put aside the wishing and start getting real about who we are and what we're good at. I've never met anyone who doesn't excel at anything. Everyone has something they're good at—it's just a matter of figuring out how it fits into your life.

So really focus your attention on the things at which you excel. Begin by assessing your personal strengths and then get on a path that will take full advantage of them. Be completely and always honest with yourself, and the rest will follow.

Acceptance of Self

Why is it so difficult for people to accept who they really are? In a word, *pressure*. There's so much pressure, especially in today's hyper-competitive and hyper-informed society, for people to be something they're not. We get it from parents, from friends, from spouses, from television, from the Internet, from magazines, from advertisements we pass in the street, from nearly everything we see and do in any given day.

These factors have bred a culture that never seems satisfied with anything. And that dissatisfaction makes itself known when you're very young. You could be an extraordinary painter as a child, but then everyone wants to know why you're not an exceptional singer. If you're a musician, why not an athlete? If you're an athlete, why not an honor student? If you're an honor student, why not a social butterfly? And the list goes on and on. All this pressure leads to the destructive tendency to compete with others, as outlined in step one.

But it also leads to an equally destructive tendency to compete not with ourselves but with the versions of our ideal selves that our culture has created in our minds. The result is that we can never truly work on bettering ourselves because we're always comparing ourselves to the ideal. Every race, background, and age group deals with wishing they were somebody else. Too many of us, instead of embracing who we are and working on maximizing our talents, fall into the trap of trying to be a different sort of individual from the one we were destined to be.

The surest way to break this cycle is to stop conforming to the rules of everything. Many of my interviewees got to where they are today primarily because they chose to do something completely different from the norm. I was the same way. I always made my own style. I always befriended people who weren't the status quo. And when it came time to pursue my career, I would pursue an almost comically polar opposite from whatever was expected of me. In nearly all instances, I would do exactly the opposite of what people told me I needed to do. And as a result, I have found success.

Now, I don't necessarily advocate always doing the exact opposite of what's expected. Rather I return to my advice about looking in the mirror. See who you are. *Really* see it. And when you have seen it, adopt an attitude that you're not afraid to go against the grain. Stop adapting to society and start being yourself. The empowerment that results will astonish you.

3. **Understand that you are in control.**
There is nothing in this world you don't control—both internally and externally. Sure, you can't influence the direction of massive things like international policy, but you can dictate how much that policy affects you internally. No matter how much influence an external factor might have on the people around you, the self-actualized remain unaffected. This is because they know exactly who they are and can therefore always adapt—and do so quickly. Because they do not lie to themselves about

their own identities, strengths, and weaknesses, they have immediate and clear pictures of the adjustments they need to make to render the external factors irrelevant.

When a business suffers a cash flow shortfall, the self-actualized know exactly how to find the resources they need to get by. When a policy change at work makes the path to promotion less likely, the self-actualized know how to alter the path and ensure continued upward movement. When a recession hits, the self-actualized find ways to continue their lives as if nothing has changed.

Understand that the power you possess in terms of your outlook is absolutely astonishing. If you are realistic, honest, and above all authentic, there is nothing you can't achieve.

4. Don't stop growing.

Perhaps the only flaw in Maslow's hierarchy of needs is that it is presented as a pyramid. Pyramids have peaks. They have endpoints. But those who self-actualize understand that the journey is never over. This is exactly why all twelve of the women interviewed for this book said they were not yet self-actualized. To self-actualize requires self-awareness, and self-awareness requires an understanding that there is no such thing as a finished product. There is no such thing as perfection and no such thing as an endgame. To be self-actualized is to understand that you must never stop growing as a person and learning as a professional.

When asked about whether she had self-actualized, Bobbie Kelsey-Grayson, head coach of the University of Wisconsin's women's basketball team, said: "I don't think I'm there yet, but I'm much further than I was when I first started out. I'm striving to get there, always evolving and learning." When asked how she might evolve and learn as a coach, she instead highlighted other life pursuits. "I want to learn Italian. I want to be a piano player. I'd like to learn carpentry. There are a hundred things like that I'll need to learn before I can ever call myself self-actualized."

This is the point in a nutshell: the first huge part of self-actualization is accepting your true self, but the second huge part is understanding that the journey has no endpoint. There is no destination. To self-actualize you must always strive to expand your horizons as a human being. To achieve success you must always seek it.

In closing I would like to share how strange an experience it was to write a chapter on self-actualization as if I am an authority on the subject. After all, like my twelve counterparts I interviewed for this book, I recognize that I have not yet self-actualized. But this is the important part: I understand that I am on my way. Anyone who has visited my website or read about my background or seen even one of my Twitter posts should recognize that I have accepted who I am and have come to embrace my strengths and weaknesses. I am on the path to self-actualization not because I read Maslow's book but because I have learned how to focus on my core competencies rather than reach for every passing star that comes by; because I have accepted the people who love me genuinely instead of reaching out or changing myself to please the people I want to love me; because I have learned to like myself for who I truly am; because I have come to realize we only have so much time on this earth and, no matter my background, I must work to maximize my time here; because—and this is perhaps the most important part—I would rather spend day after day enhancing who I am than even one moment wondering why I'm not doing something else.

Self-actualization does not require any tricks or tools. To reach this level of the hierarchy, you need only accept who you are and then take the steps necessary to become the best version of you that you can be. Once you are 110-percent comfortable with who you are, who you've surrounded yourself with, and what you're destined to do on this earth, you may begin your journey toward self-actualization. Just know the journey never ends; no matter what you achieve, there is always plenty more that awaits. It might seem daunting at first glance, but when you have come to realize all these things, the journey will become a most pleasant experience.

Inspire Others

Brainy, Brave, Bubbly, Benevolent

We have reached the point in the book when it's time to begin thinking about what to do once you have found that success. One of the surest ways to be branded the B word, after all, is to reach the top and never look back. So few people achieve the pinnacles of their careers, and even fewer manage to create profitable and sustainable businesses. If you have realized either of these elusive dreams, it is time to begin thinking about how to give back. Many books on the topic of business development and entrepreneurship would suggest matters of charity, and I would not disagree that financial contributions to the community benefit not only others but the giver himself or herself. But what I would like to discuss in this chapter is an initiative that costs the giver little more than time. You have reached the top. Yes, give back to your community. But also do everything you can to be an inspiration to others.

It seems safe to assume that since you are reading this book you are the kind of person who looks for inspiration from others. Maybe you had a mentor at a young age. Maybe there was a teacher who inspired you. Maybe something happened in your life that inspired you to better yourself. Maybe you saw something on television or read a book—maybe even this book—that inspired you to greatness. Having achieved that greatness, now it is time to repay the favor. You are at the top of your game. You are approaching the point of self-actualization. You have everything you need in life. Now it is time to share your wisdom with the people who need it. Now is the time to mentor the folks who hope to follow in your footsteps.

When I think about inspiration, what inspires me most is ordinary people who have done extraordinary things. I appreciate when someone has the ability and willingness to be selfless, creative, or innovative, or just dares to be different. Mother Teresa. Gandhi. Martin Luther King, Jr. All of them were ordinary people who decided the world needed their help—true leaders who believed they could change the world and who, despite nearly impossible odds and tremendous opposition, weren't afraid to try.

The beautiful thing about inspiration of this kind is that *ordinary* part. Certainly each of these people had that charismatic ability to lead others to better things. But all of them came from backgrounds of great poverty and difficulty. All of them faced giant mountains to climb. They managed to reach the summits of those mountains not simply because they were great leaders but because they were not afraid to be who they were. They were authentic. And they demanded authenticity in those who followed them as well.

It's amazing to me how often people who do great things tend to downplay their own ability to inspire. "I'm just good with marketing," someone will say. "That's all I know. I have nothing else to offer." Never mind that the marketing skill in question launched a lifelong business; the typical reaction people have when asked if they are inspiring is to downplay their inspirational achievements and qualities. Call it humility. Call it narrow-mindedness. Call it whatever you like. What it means is that too many of us fail to see the greatness within ourselves. Too many of us assume a person is only great if he or she makes national headlines. But press isn't necessary. In fact sometimes the most inspiring people in the world go completely unnoticed. What inspires are the people who do something to better humanity in their own small corner of the world. They don't need headlines or accolades. They need only to know they stepped up to make things better.

Consider Tai Beauchamp's story. Tai is a style expert and national correspondent for *InStyle* magazine, and when I asked her what inspired her, she didn't list famous names. She listed mentors. Brave people who rose above the odds to help shape her into the dynamic woman and successful entrepreneur she has become.

"My grandmother was raising her children while working and going to college at the same time," Tai said. "And then she found out that her sixteen-year-old was pregnant. 'Okay, fine,' she said. 'We're having a baby.' I can't even imagine the strength and courage it took to continue on like that."

The bravery didn't end there either. Despite being a teenage mother, Tai's mother went on to college and worked to help pay the bills all the while. Her mother and grandmother eventually went on to graduate school, obtaining their master's degrees and instilling in Tai a sense of the importance of education along the way. "My mom and grandma have been testaments to my life and perseverance. They inspired me because they showed me you don't have to take life lying down."

Understand that you can be an inspiration to others no matter what you feel you have or have not achieved. As discussed in the previous chapter, part of the compulsion to be an entrepreneur or to climb the ladder at work—part of that initiative to self-actualize—is an unwillingness to believe that the journey has reached its end. The most successful among us are the people who are never satisfied with what they have already achieved. But don't confuse that drive with an unworthiness to inspire. Even if you feel you have not yet reached the endpoint, and even if you feel like you have reached a low point, you have the ability to inspire.

Consider trainer and business consultant Ana Cortés. "When I moved to Phoenix, I was alone," she explained as she described her circuitous path to success as a business owner. "I didn't know anyone. I was still trying to connect myself to the community when I learned I had already become an inspiration. One day someone called me and said, 'We want to feature you as one of the forty most influential women under forty.'"

The request came as quite a shock to Ana. "That was the point where I asked myself what they were seeing that I wasn't seeing. That was the point where I realized I had to move forward and make something happen for someone else."

For Ana the chance to mentor and to inspire others has been a gift and a blessing that she no longer takes for granted. The question you have to ask yourself upon achieving your success is: will you do the same?

To Give or Not to Give?

How much is too much success? Is it possible to keep too much of it for yourself? Of course. The strange thing is that many people who reach the top of the mountain don't even think about turning back around to help others up the path. And there is no good reason for this. Giving back not only helps the people around you; it can actually benefit you and your business as well. It's truly a win-win: you wind up feeling good about yourself for helping others, the people you help will be closer to achieving their goals, and the community at large, upon recognizing your charity, will think of you and your business in a higher regard.

Recall for a moment the list of personal attributes gained during the esteem tier of Maslow's hierarchy of needs: self-esteem, confidence, achievement, respect of others, and respect by others. Knowing that list, is there a surer way to surmount the esteem tier than giving back to the community and working to inspire others? To be able to stand flat-footed in front of someone in need and tell them honestly how and why you have done what you have done—and, more importantly, share with them exactly how they can do it now—is the epitome of self-actualization. Certainly there are external rewards for giving and mentoring, but the internal rewards far outweigh any of them. To give is to demonstrate to yourself that you have come full circle; it is a representation of your achievement and an affirmation of all you have accomplished.

For a business owner, giving back to the community and inspiring others improves the business's reputation. It can lead to more customers and more referrals as a result. The company's profile will receive a boost. And the community at large becomes better as well. For nine-to-fivers, giving back helps broaden horizons and allows them to achieve beyond the walls of their own offices. While they have given a great deal of themselves to their employers, they may now give back to something greater than themselves. It represents a holistic growth made possible by the career growth the nine-to-fiver has worked so tirelessly to achieve.

No matter who you are, giving back and inspiring others comes equipped with many benefits. You never know who you're going to impact when you give—and you never know who might be in a position to reciprocate if you ever find yourself in a time of need. Giving back leaves a legacy that will live on far longer than you will. And you will be amazed by the way inspiring others makes you feel. In fact it is the only feeling that rivals the one you get when you realize you have achieved your dream.

No Financing

Many times people are hesitant to give back because they assume it will cost too much. The kind of inspiration and aid we're talking about in this chapter has nothing to do with money. In fact the greatest inspiration often comes from the volunteering not of funds but of time. Never underestimate the power of offering your wisdom through conversation. Your thoughts and wisdom are bound to help people far more than your checkbook ever could. Sometimes just listening is the greatest way to exact change.

For the successful person, sometimes the key skills that led to that success are the best things to share. Business owners got to where they are in part because they were such good planners and organizers—people with tremendous foresight and ability to adapt to change. This lends itself nicely to helping other people create plans for themselves. Whether it's a charity to benefit the community or a person aspiring to follow in your footsteps, your planning skills are sure to be instrumental to their progress.

As an inspirational person, being supportive and encouraging is the most basic yet the most helpful thing you can do. Offer advice, offer aid, and just be there for those in need and you will affect so many positive changes that money won't even need to be a consideration.

How to Give Back and Inspire Others

By now you're well aware of the benefits that come from giving back and inspiring others. The question then becomes: how do you do it? Certainly there are many opportunities by way of existing charities and outreach programs, but on an individual level there are also a number of tips to consider when you're thinking about how you might help those around you. Embrace the following points and you will go from wanting to inspire people to actually inspiring people on a daily basis.

1. **Act and show.**
   Don't simply say you want to serve as an inspiration; get out there and do something. Commit to an initiative. Reach out to someone who has recognized you as a leader. Show people who you are as an inspiration.

   I asked the twelve women I interviewed for this book a simple question: do you consider yourself an inspiration? Without fail all of them answered like this: "I try to be." When asked how they inspire, all of them talked about the things they did for work and the things they did to help women at large see the bigger picture. Helping women to find and accept their own identities was a big call to arms for the majority of my contributors. "Being your authentic self" was certainly the most inspirational quality cited.

   It is one thing to act on that desire to serve as an inspiration, but it is entirely another to *live* as that inspiration. This all goes back to being authentic. Follow through with the things you promise. Be true to your brand. Be proud of who you are and what you have accomplished. This will inspire those around you to do the same.

2. **Provide others with the Blueprint.**
   There is a reason you have achieved all you have achieved. You had the skills, yes, but you also had the Blueprint. Now that you have reached the top, you are bound to receive requests for advice from people who hope to be just like you one day. Some

of these people you will know. Some you will not. Provided they are respectful and willing to learn, all are deserving of your time and wisdom.

When someone approaches you in search of your Blueprint—or when you do your part to relate your Blueprint to a charitable organization—be sure to share with them fully everything you can remember about what led to your success. Tell stories. Share your experiences. Relate your trials and tribulations. Offer your best advice. Don't hold anything back. Doing this will allow you to make a mark on someone's life and on the world at large in ways you never could have dreamed possible. It's kind of like when you have a child and for the first time realize there is something in this world more important than you. Watching someone you have helped achieve success is a feeling akin to watching your child succeed. It's a feeling that will far surpass the happiness you enjoyed when you reached the top.

3. **Become a mentor.**
One of the greatest ways to inspire is to serve as a mentor, but not all mentor-mentee relationships make sense. When considering someone to mentor, you have to make sure your background and experience aligns with what she hopes to achieve. More importantly you have to ready yourself to be completely open and honest. When people look at you as a mentor, they believe in you completely. If you aren't totally authentic in your advice to them, you are doing them a disservice.

Further you must be selfless. There will be times when your instincts will influence you to hold back on certain tips and advice that helped you reach the top. That's your competitive spirit getting in the way. Other times you will hold back on things because you feel it won't help your mentee. Resist these urges. If you're truly great at what you do, you know a hundred and one more ways to do something without having to worry about giving away knowledge.

At the same time, don't give away too much. While it is important not to hold back on the things your mentee will need to succeed, it is also important to allow her opportunities to learn things for herself. Sometimes mistakes are the best lessons. Remember, your job is to make things clearer for your mentee, not to do her job for her. Mentoring isn't about hand-holding; it is about helping your mentees stay on the right path.

Sometimes to volunteer is to mentor. Look for different groups or organizations to whose initiatives you might lend your wisdom. These organizations might address a field similar to your own. They might provide outreach to people who remind you of yourself when you were younger and less successful. When searching for a sensible organization to align with, travel back in your mind to a time when you were an aspiring entrepreneur or business leader. The person you see in your mind is the kind of person you should be trying to mentor.

Allow me to leave you with one final important note: you might be thinking the only time in your life when you can inspire is when you have achieved your dream. That is simply not so. No matter how far along you are on the path to greatness, you are farther along than someone else. This person could certainly use your help and advice. To this person you can be a great inspiration. So when it comes time to give back, there is never a better time than now.

Stay Ahead of the Curve

Buoyant, Bouncy, Buyer, Bookworm, Bloomer

Economically speaking, the world has seen better days. The strange and interesting thing about humanity—at least in terms of how it relates to economic trends—is that it so often fails to learn lessons from its own history. The recession that began in late 2008 is certainly not the first, and it surely isn't going to be the last. Yet so many among us were surprised by the notion that we could possibly tumble into the darkest economic period since the Great Depression. You know what's true about those people who were surprised? They, like millions of others who lost their savings or their jobs during the downturn, wouldn't have been surprised—and could have avoided disaster as a result—if they had managed to stay ahead of the curve.

That's the point at which we have arrived in this chapter. Prior to this page, you learned many high-powered strategies that will help you reach the top. But perhaps the most important lessons you can take away from this book are those that will help you to *stay there*. One of the most common themes among the contributors to this book is the notion that success isn't an endpoint. You can never stop evolving or learning. You can't get too high or too low. You can't get comfortable. The moment you relax a little, or the moment you get caught up in the excitement about what seems at the time to be a good thing, is the moment you begin losing money, losing business, or regressing in your goals.

Think about it. One of the primary truths we know about life is that change is constant. What is true today may not be true tomorrow. The trend last year will most assuredly not be the trend this year. Your computer? Obsolete in six months. The book you might be holding? It's getting overtaken by the e-reader version. That e-reader you might be holding? There will be a better one out soon. It could be that the entire format will one day be replaced by something even quicker, lower-cost, and more convenient. We see it all around us. Trends shift. Things are constantly being developed. The way consumers view and buy things can change practically overnight. Further, each generation is different from the last. Your grandfather might look at a computer as if it were the most perplexing thing he's ever seen while your three-year-old daughter might be able to create her own web page in a matter of hours.

Back to the economy. We are where we are at the time of this writing for one reason: we failed to recognize that change is inevitable. More importantly we failed to see how the vast changes in technology would lead to a different brand of consumerism in almost every industry. We failed to see that commerce has become truly global. Many who lost their jobs did so because they failed to reinvent themselves and gain the knowledge necessary to remain competitive in this new global market. Many who lost their homes did so because they believed that the wisdoms that were true for their parents and grandparents would remain true today.

Not so. Twenty years ago working hard as a lone strategy made sense. As long as you showed up on time, worked harder than the other guy, and always did your job, you'd always have your job. But as technology has changed and the world has become smaller, the boundaries of the competition have become incredibly vast. These have been difficult times for millions, but the vast majority of those millions are experiencing difficulty because they did not adapt to this brave new world. They did not keep up with the demands of the times. They did not stay ahead of the curve.

"You can't fight the change," Dina Marto of Twelve Music Group told me—and she would know better than most, given that she has been in the industry long enough to have weathered the Napster fallout and the subsequent iTunes revolution. If you want to see a sector that looks absolutely nothing like it did twenty years ago, you don't need to look much further than music. Remember the booming record store chains of the '90s? Gone. Remember those vast aisles of CDs you would see in big-box electronic stores? Downsized. They used to consume nearly half of the in-store space; now they occupy maybe an aisle or two near the checkout line. Not long ago albums drove the success or failure of these big-box stores. They were the top-ticket items. Now the only place you can find them is on small shelves near the checkout aisle.

"Technology—and in particular iTunes—has changed the game in my industry," Dina shared. "The companies that survived the transition were the ones that figured out the best way to roll with the punches." Just as importantly Dina reminded me that change is constant. Even though Twelve Music Group was founded after the most significant wave of change in the music industry's history, that doesn't mean it can get comfortable. Still more change is coming.

In many ways dramatic changes occur as often as news breaks. "I try to stay current with what's happening in the world because music is so influenced by societal issues. Art imitates life. Life imitates art." Her best advice for staying ahead of the curve? "Keep your ears to the streets. Just make sure you're always on the ground level of everything you do."

Remember Blockbuster? There was a time when it seemed like you could find one in every neighborhood of every city. They became a giant of a company because their model was brilliant at the time. Where other mom-and-pop movie rental stores had to deal with the reality of occasionally having to tell their customers they were out of stock on a popular item, Blockbuster provided its popular new releases in such bulk that sellouts were rarely an issue. They further revolutionized the industry by extending the period a person could expect to keep that new release without being charged late fees. They created customer loyalty programs, began selling used videos, expanded into video game rentals, and began forming tie-ins with film production companies looking to promote upcoming releases. At its peak Blockbuster was the name of the game in movie rental.

But Blockbuster failed to stay ahead of the curve. While its competition was looking for ways to exploit the flaws in the Blockbuster model, Blockbuster itself hung back and remained content with its existing model. Companies like Redbox came in with the idea that people would value the time-saving convenience of never again having to wait in one of those occasionally epic lines at Blockbuster over the guarantee that the movie they were hoping to see is in stock. It turned out they were right. Now you see a Redbox outside almost every grocery store in America.

Then came Netflix, a modern-day online behemoth of a company making the movie rental service even simpler. Instead of having to drive all the way to the neighborhood Blockbuster, the user could just make a few clicks online and then find the video waiting for them in their mailbox a day or two later. What could be simpler than that? As Netflix taught us, it turns out that streaming the videos directly on the Internet is simpler. Even the company that changed the video rental game proved a strong ability to adapt. The result has been a revolution in how we consume movies and television in the United States. The other result has been the near-death of Blockbuster, the one-time titan of video rental.

As you can see, a failure to stay ahead of the curve can have devastating consequences for the individual, the company (no matter how successful), and even the country and the economy. No one is immune to the awesome power of change. Only those who learn to stay on top of the news, properly identify future trends, network for the future, and absorb and adapt to the latest technology can hope to survive in any economy or through any major industry change.

How to Stay Ahead of the Curve

As you ponder your own success, keep in mind the things that helped you to reach the top in the first place. Just because the world is constantly changing, that does not mean the things that made you great might soon be irrelevant. It also doesn't mean the philosophies outlined in this book can be thrown out the window. The strategies you have learned in these pages work in almost any business setting and will always be valuable in helping you to position your business in the market or yourself in your chosen career. That said, we know change is inevitable and success is only constant if you work at making it so. Consider, then, the following strategies an addendum of sorts—a guide for how to ensure you and your company change with the times while never abandoning the things that make you great.

1. **Keep up with technology.**
    This might seem like an obvious point, but it's shocking to me how many once-proud companies have fallen in the past decade simply because they didn't fully grasp how new technologies threatened their underlying business models. For as quickly as technology changes, it's astonishing how slowly some people adapt. There are some major corporations still installing reasonable e-mail systems while their competition is creating apps for the iPad.

    Some companies fail to keep up with technology because they refuse to believe their hundred-year-old business model can ever be challenged. Consider the publishing industry. Even though the writing has been on the wall for years, major publishing companies are only just now starting to figure out how to evolve toward the e-reader model.

    So how can you avoid a similar fate—especially considering the incredibly rapid rate of change in the realm of technology? There are a few key strategies for you to consider. First, and this will be a common theme throughout these steps, it always helps to talk about technology with someone who is younger than you. If you're fifty or sixty, try to be patient with the younger people you speak to, as they will be telling you about things that might seem quite foreign. And even if you're twenty-five, don't assume you have all the answers. There are technologies emerging that you've not yet heard of—technologies that most assuredly gained a foothold due to popularity with people twenty and under.

So, no matter your age, be sure to include in your network a trusted confidante who is younger than you. Consider an entry-level coworker. Consider a college student you know. Consider your children, if you have them. As time goes by, be sure always to consult with someone in that lowest age demographic. When it comes to the biggest and most important new technology trends, they know best.

Subscribing to trade magazines is always a good idea. Mainstream technology magazines often help too. These publications are always on the cutting edge of what's fresh and what's coming out in the technology realm. As an added bonus, they sometimes provide insight into what your competition is doing with technology—and that always helps illustrate how to stay ahead of the curve.

No matter what your job or business, constantly looking for ways to expand your knowledge base and expertise is always a sound strategy. Cross-training and earning new certifications will keep you relevant at work. Seminars will keep you in the know as a business leader. And becoming proficient in the latest technologies will always ensure you're never passed up by someone who knows something you don't.

Where technology goes, that is where the consumer goes. Think of the highest-profile companies in the world today. Google, Facebook, Amazon. They got there because they were furthest ahead of the curve when it mattered. They will remain there as long as they continue to adapt to new trends and capitalize on every opportunity presented by new technology. If you don't know how to use a new technology, it's always best practice to learn. Even if it represents a couple hundred or even a couple thousand dollar investment, it will be worth it in the end.

2. **Enhance your marketability.**
As you learned in earlier chapters, brand is king. Like technology companies, brands must always stay fresh if they are going to survive. You already know the importance of cross-training, of staying abreast of what's going on in the market, and of focusing most of your energy on the markets that matter. But have you considered adding on to your core competencies?

One of the surest ways to ensure your customers don't start straying to the competition—or your employers don't start thinking of other candidates for that promotion—is to expand on the number of items or services you offer and the number of things you're qualified to do. In my marketing career, I began with consultations, writing business plans, and creating strategies. As I built my customer base, I kept them loyal by branching out into research, promotion strategy, brainstorming, and more. With my universities I began by teaching courses from existing coursework, but now I'm expanding by offering the ability to create courses and design rubrics.

The bottom line is I'm doing more than one thing in my field. In so doing I'm offering more than the competition. You can do this too, no matter what line of work you find yourself in. It's not always the core product that keeps the clients happy. It's the little extras that count. That's a great way to stay ahead of the curve.

To Thine Own Self Be True

Notice that in step two, I mentioned expanding on your core competencies, not replacing them. The quickest way to ensure loss of business—quicker even than falling behind the curve—is to stop offering the services or items that brought the customers in the door in the first place.

"Staying ahead of the curve only works if I stay true to myself and my craft," celebrity photographer Drexina Nelson informed me. "People come to me because they seek my vision and my eye. It's not about falling into what's popular. It's about staying true to my original vision."

Drexina makes an excellent point. While staying ahead of the curve is incredibly important, the effort is of little value if you abandon your principles along the way. You became a success for a reason. You have to stay true to yourself if you hope to remain a success. This process is about evolution, not replacement. Drexina became one of the hottest photographers in Atlanta because she shoots beauty and fashion like nobody else. She continues to evolve as a photographer by keeping up with the latest technologies and techniques, but the strength of her art remains the same.

———

3. Use social media to its fullest.

I'm still shocked by the number of people who think social media isn't necessary in today's world. Facebook, Twitter, and LinkedIn are household names for a reason: they're great services, and hundreds of millions of people use them. Why would anyone want to pass up a captured audience of millions? The idea seems insane.

It doesn't matter if you think of your company as a cutting-edge movement or a button-down firm; there is opportunity to be had via social networking. I wouldn't be writing this book today if not for the followings I have managed to build on Facebook and Twitter. Remember, every friend or follower is a potential lead—for a sale, for a business contact, or simply for a chance to get ahead. You don't turn down potential leads in the real world. Why would you turn them down in the social networking sphere?

For those who realize the power in social networking, there are a number of important things to consider as you attempt to maximize your network. First, Google yourself every day. There's a popular saying floating around online that goes like this: if you're not on Google, you don't exist. I would like to add to that this piece of advice: if the message about you on Google isn't what you want it to be, you must take steps to change it. Sometimes the best way to track your own performance is to see what anonymous users are saying about you online. The stark honesty that often shows up in these environments can be a tremendous help in righting wrongs and fixing weaknesses. The most important thing is that you want as many Google hits as possible, and of those hits you want as much positive and on-point feedback as you can get.

When it comes time to create or expand your Facebook presence or your Twitter following, consider the following rules that have led to my own success. First, always use discretion when posting something online, whether it's personal or professional in nature. Your online presence is your brand manifested on millions of computer screens. How many people really care about what you had for lunch? If you can count the number on one hand, you shouldn't post about it. Post only the things that are most relevant to the expansion and awareness of your brand.

Second, always offer *information*. It should speak directly to the definition of your brand. If you're in IT, for example, you should post wisdom, offer quotes, and link to articles about IT. I'm in marketing, so nearly everything I post online has to do with my core marketing principles. Third, as you attempt to make new connections, concentrate on people in your field. It's just like building the right network. You don't want to befriend everyone on Facebook and Twitter—just the people who really make sense for your circle. If you concentrate only on aligning yourself with key people, it eliminates the clutter in your following and also ensures growth happens only in those areas where you desire it.

The benefits of social networking are staggering. People are more open and honest on the Internet, so if you can gain a significant following, you will have a better feel for what people really want. It's the best way to remain informed about current and evolving trends. And it's a wonderful (and free!) way to stay connected.

4. **Talk to, associate with, and hire young people.** I've already alluded to this point, but nobody has their finger on the pulse of change more than young people. Nearly all trends in business and in life happen from the bottom up in the demographic

scale. Especially in matters of technology and culture, young people hold the key.

"I'm always learning and training," business consultant Ana Cortés shared, "but I often get a great deal of my knowledge from people who are younger than I am. I'm always looking for people who are smarter than me. Always looking for younger and more creative people. They might not have as much experience as I do, but in many ways they can share the wisdom to see things I don't see."

This was a common theme among all twelve interviewees. Yes, it is important to celebrate your own strengths, but it's just as important to know what you don't know. Staying ahead of the curve is a matter of learning what you don't know, and the best way to do that is to embrace your knowledge deficits and reach out to people who can help fill them. Where experts fall short or prove inaccessible, young people can often do just that. Young people are creative, energetic, and in the know about trends. Why wouldn't they be of help to your business?

Whether you're in business for yourself or working for someone else, there is no such thing as 100 percent job security. The best way to make sure your percentage of retaining your position or your success remains high is to stay ahead of the curve. For the nine-to-fiver, be sure to take advantage of every opportunity to expand your education. Cross-train whenever you can. Learn new disciplines. Make yourself useful in a wider range of tasks. Show your employer you can manage any task they throw at you without the need for any handholding.

For the entrepreneur, make sure you're always evolving as a company. Offer new things. Adapt to new technologies. Expand your brand. Diversify your customer base. Doing these things ensures you're more immune to downsizing during economic downturns. It also ensures you can survive on other resources should an entire sector of your client base dry up.

We have come now to the end of the final rule. And with that I leave you with this critical piece of advice: above all else, never settle. If you work hard, stick to your blueprint, and follow the wisdom shared in this book, you will find success eventually. But if you are a truly empowered entrepreneur or nine-to-fiver, you will soon see that in business there is really no endpoint. If you're in business, you have to understand that your customers' needs are constantly changing. If you're employed by someone else, you have to understand that in order to move up, you have to keep evolving as an employee. Keep in mind that your competitors are working hard to innovate the next big thing every day. If you hope to avoid becoming obsolete, you must consistently offer variations of your products or services. If you're not evolving, you're dying. I always tell my clients that marketing is a long-term investment. So too is maintaining success.

The Journey Is the Destination

"I once wrote an article for TechCrunch that mentioned how surprised I was when I realized that, after I sold my company, I still wanted to keep going." These were the words of Prerna Gupta, the serial entrepreneur currently heading the music app company Khush. "Before I got started on that company, I had a goal of reaching ten million users and then selling my company so I could make enough money to retire and live on a beach and surf all day. When I sold my company back in December [2011], I had pretty much reached all of those goals. But what was shocking to me was that, rather than wanting to retire, I was already working on the next thing. My original goal was ten million users. Now it's a hundred million."

There's a great lesson in this for any aspiring or current entrepreneur. If you follow the wisdoms provided in this book—and if you truly live them—you *will* reach your goals. It might happen next year, it might happen next week, or it might happen in the next decade, but you *will* reach them. That's the funny thing about the business spirit. It's what Prerna calls "both a blessing and a trap." "It would not be good to just reach your goal and say, 'That's it. I'm done.' You have to keep concentrating on something that drives you forward."

Given that we began our journey together with a chapter on goals, it seems only appropriate that we should end on the same subject. That's the thing about evolution: many of the best growth moments in life have a tendency to deliver you full circle. You have a goal. You achieve it. You establish a new goal. You achieve it. And the journey continues. This is the only way to truly grow.

When I first sat down to write this book, my goal was simply to finish. When I finished, I made it my goal to improve it to the point where it would be the best book I could possibly write. Now that I have come to the end of my journey in this respect, I could not be prouder of what I have managed to produce, but at the same time I am continuing my path as a thought leader and businesswoman. I still have work to do. I have achieved my goal to write my first book, but there are still dozens of goals left to accomplish. And when those are done, there will be dozens more.

Congratulations are in order for the steps you have taken toward your personal success story. Always remember you are a powerful woman. You are so much more than any one B word could ever describe. You are Bright. Brilliant. Beautiful. Brave. Thanks to all your strengths—and with an assist from the wisdoms provided by the thirteen contributors (myself included) to this book—you are well on your way to success. Remember, though, that when you achieve that success, you have not in fact reached the endpoint. Life is a constant and ever-evolving journey. Work hard and achieve, and by all means be sure to enjoy your success along the way. Celebrate your successes, but always look toward the future, never give up on your dreams, and be sure to realize your ultimate vision.

Dr. R. Kay Green is the CEO and president of RKG Marketing Solutions, Inc. and works in online education as a professor and course developer for West Virginia University, Embry-Riddle University, University of California—Irvine, Arcadia University, and the Florida Institute of Technology, where she has taught more than 350 classes. Dr. Kay, who holds an associate's degree in marketing management, a bachelor's in administration in marketing, a MBA in marketing and management, and a doctorate of business administration in marketing, has been featured on Great Women Speakers, Black Experts, and Guru.com.

www.ivebeencalledthebword.com

www.ingramcontent.com/pod-product-compliance
Lightning Source LLC
Chambersburg PA
CBHW071944090426
42740CB00011B/1808